REFLECTIONS *by* *fidel*

REFLECTIONS by *fidel*

PUBLISHING BUREAU
OF THE COUNCIL OF STATE

Creative Group & Information Office
of the Council of State

ISBN 978-959-274-050-1

© About the present edition: *Office of Publications of the Council*
of State of the Republic of Cuba.
Calle 17 número 552, esquina a D,
Vedado, Havana, Cuba.
Tel: (537) 55-1858,
Fax: (537) 57 4578

MORE THAN THREE BILLION
PEOPLE IN THE WORLD ARE BEING
CONDEMNED TO A PREMATURE
DEATH FROM HUNGER
AND THIRST

t is not an exaggeration; this is rather a conservative figure. I have meditated for quite a long time on that after the meeting held by President Bush with the US automakers.

«The sinister idea of turning foodstuffs into fuel was definitely established as the economic strategy of the US foreign policy»

The sinister idea of turning foodstuffs into fuel was definitely established as the economic strategy of the US foreign policy on Monday, March 26th last.

A wire service issued by the AP, a US information agency with worldwide coverage, literally reads:

«WASHINGTON (AP), March 26 - President Bush touted the benefits of flexible fuel» vehicles running on ethanol and biodiesel on Monday, meeting with automakers to boost support for his energy plans. Bush said a commitment by the leaders of the domestic auto industry to double their production of flex-fuel vehicles could help motorists shift away from gasoline and reduce the nation's reliance on imported oil.

« "That's a major technological breakthrough for the country" » Bush said after inspecting three alternative vehicles. If the nation wants to reduce gasoline use, he said the consumer has got to be in a position to make a rational choice.

»The president urged Congress to move expeditiously on legislation the administration recently proposed to require the use of 35 billion gallons of alternative fuels by 2017 and seek higher fuel economy standards for automobiles.

»Bush met with General Motors Corp. chairman and chief executive Rick Wagoner, Ford Motor Co. chief executive Alan Mulally and DaimlerChrysler AG's Chrysler Group chief executive Tom LaSorda. They discussed support for flex-fuel vehicles, attempts to develop ethanol from alternative sources like switchgrass and wood chips and the administration's proposal to reduce gas consumption by 20 percent in 10 years.

»The discussions came amid rising gasoline prices. The latest Lundberg Survey found the nationwide average for gasoline has risen 6 cents per gallon in the past two weeks to $2.61».

I think that reducing and recycling all fuel and electricity operated engines is an urgent and elemental necessity of all humanity. The dilemma is not in the reduction of energy costs, but in the idea of turning foodstuffs into fuel.

Today we know with accurate precision that one ton of corn can only render as an average 413 liters of ethanol (109 gallons), a figure that may vary according to the latter's density.

The average price of corn in US ports has reached 167 dollars per ton. The production of 35 billion gallons of ethanol requires 320 million tons of corn.

According to FAO, US corn production in 2005 reached 280.2 million tons.

Even if the President is speaking about producing fuel out of switchgrass or wood chips, any person could understand that these phrases are far from realistic. Listen well: 35 billion gallons, 35 followed by nine zeros!

Beautiful examples of the productivity of men per hectare achieved by the experienced and well organized US farmers

A ton of corn can be used to produce a mere 413 litres of ethanol on average

will come next: corn will be turned into ethanol; corn wastes will be turned into animal fodder, with a 26 percent of proteins; cattle manure will be used as raw material for the production of gas. Of course, all of this will happen after a great number of investments, which could only be afforded by the most powerful companies whose operations are based on the consumption of electricity and fuel. Let this formula be applied to the Third World countries, and the world will see how many hungry people on this planet will cease to consume corn. What is worse, let the poor countries receive some financing to produce ethanol from corn or any other foodstuff and very soon not a single tree will be left standing to protect humanity from climate change.

Other rich countries have planned to use not only corn but also wheat, sunflower seeds, rapeseed and other foodstuffs to produce fuel. For Europeans, for example, it would be a good business to import the entire soybean production of the world to reduce the cost of fuel for their automobiles and feed their animals with the wastes of that legume, which has a high content of all kinds of essential amino acids.

«Let the poor countries receive some financing to produce ethanol from corn or any other foodstuff and very soon not a single tree will be left standing to protect humanity from climate change»

In Cuba, alcohol was produced as a sugar cane by-product, after three extractions of sugarcane juice. Climate change is already affecting our sugar production. Severe droughts alternate with record rainfall values, which hardly allow our country to produce any sugar during a period of 100 days with adequate yields during our very mild winter. So, in Cuba, we are either producing less sugar per every ton of sugarcane, or the number of tons of cane per hectare has been reduced due to the long lasting droughts in the plantation and harvest seasons.

I understand that Venezuela would not export alcohol; it will use it to improve the environmental safety of its own fuel. Therefore, despite the excellent technology designed by Brazil to produce alcohol, its use in Cuba to produce alcohol from sugarcane juice is nothing but a dream, the ravings of those who entertain such ideas. In our country, the land which would otherwise be devoted solely to the production of alcohol could be better used to produce foodstuffs for the people and protect the environment.

All countries of the world without exception, whether rich or poor, could save trillions of dollars in investments and fuel if they only replace all incandescent bulbs with fluorescent bulbs, which is what Cuba has done in all the residential areas of the country. This would be a palliative that will enable us to cope with climate change without killing the poor people in this planet with hunger.

As can be seen, I am not using adjectives to describe either the system or those who have become the owners of this world.

14

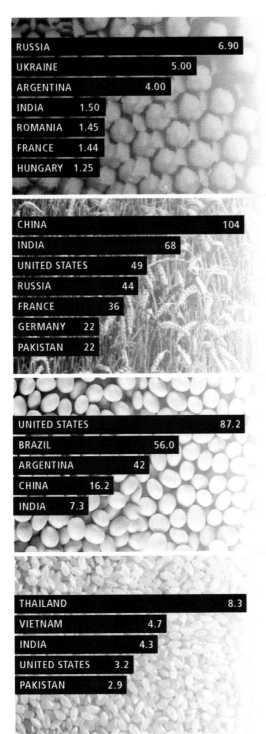

RUSSIA	6.90
UKRAINE	5.00
ARGENTINA	4.00
INDIA	1.50
ROMANIA	1.45
FRANCE	1.44
HUNGARY	1.25

SUNFLOWER SEED

Countries which produce the greatest
quantities of sunflower seed,
in millions of metric tons - 2007.

CHINA	104
INDIA	68
UNITED STATES	49
RUSSIA	44
FRANCE	36
GERMANY	22
PAKISTAN	22

WHEAT

Countries which produce the greatest
quantities of wheat,
in millions of metric tons - 2007.

UNITED STATES	87.2
BRAZIL	56.0
ARGENTINA	42
CHINA	16.2
INDIA	7.3

SOY BEAN

Countries which produce the greatest
quantities of soy bean,
in millions of metric tons (expected) -2007.

THAILAND	8.3
VIETNAM	4.7
INDIA	4.3
UNITED STATES	3.2
PAKISTAN	2.9

RICE

Countries which produce the greatest
quantities of rice, in millions
of metric tons -2006 - 2007 fiscal year.

Source: US Foreign Agricultural Services

«In our country, the land which would otherwise be devoted solely to the production of alcohol could be better used to produce foodstuffs for the people and protect the environment»

That task will be brilliantly accomplished by the information experts, the many honest socio-economic and political scientists in this world who continuously delve into the present and the future of our species. A computer and the increasing number of Internet networks will just be enough to do that.

For the first time a truly globalized economy exists and a dominant power in the economic, political, and military spheres that is in no way similar to the ancient Rome ruled by emperors.

Some people may wonder why I am speaking about hunger and thirst. And I will answer: this is not about the other side of a coin, but of the many different sides of quite another object, maybe a six-sided dice or a polyhedron which has many more sides.

This time I will quote an official news agency, founded in 1945, which is in general very familiar with the economic and social problems of the world: TELAM. It literally said:

«Within hardly 18 years, nearly 2 billion people will inhabit countries and regions where water might seem a far away memory. Two thirds of the world population could live in places where the lack of water could bring about social and economic tensions that could lead peoples to go to war over the precious "blue gold".

»In the course of the last 100 years, water consumption has grown at a pace which is more than twice the population growth rate.

HOW CLIMATE CHANGE IS AFFECTING REGIONS AROUND THE WORLD

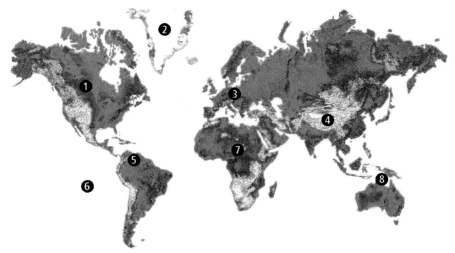

The UN report on climate change focuses on the impact of this phenomenon on 8 different regions around the world, such as the Arctic, Southern Africa, the Pacific islands and coastal regions. The most severely affected regions include:

Source: United Nations 2007

❶ North America
- More heat waves.
- More forest fires.
- Snow is constantly melting on western peaks.
- Coastal regions are threatened by floods.

❷ Polar regions
- Temperatures are on the rise, ice and glaciers are melting and flora and fauna are being affected.
- Changes in the permafrost are having an impact on infrastructure.

❸ Europe
- Growing risk of floods, especially in central and western europe.

● **Southern Europe**
- More heat waves.
- Forest fires.
- Water shortages.
- Endangered crops.

● **Northern Europe**
- Better crops.
- Increased hydraulic energy production.

❹ Asia
- Glaciar melting in Himalayas.
- Rising water levels and growing floods threats.
- Decreased precipitation is affecting crops and animal feeds production.

❺ South and Central America
- Receding tropical forests.
- Thinning savannas.
- The sea level is rising and threatening cities on the Atlantic coast.

❻ Small Pacific Islands
- Growing risk of rising sea level and storms.
- Dwindling drinking water reserves.
- Tourism threatened.

❼ Africa
- Drought, water shortages.
- Fishing and tourism threatened.
- Crops and food production affected.

❽ Australia, New Zealand
- Growing water shortages.
- More threatened species in Great Barrier Reef and other reef reservation.
- Coastal regions threatened by more storms and floods.
- Increased worldwide moderate temperatures offer New Zealand better condittions for agriculture.

«Within hardly 18 years, nearly 2 billion people will inhabit countries and regions where water might seem a far away memory»

»According to the World Water Council (WWC), the number of persons affected by this serious situation will increase to 3.5 billion by the year 2015.

»On March 23, the United Nations Organization observed the World Water Day, urging all member countries to cope with the international water shortage as of that day, under the auspices of FAO, with the aim of emphasizing the increasing importance of water shortage in the world and the need for greater integration and cooperation to ensure a sustainable and efficient management of water resources.

»Many regions in this planet suffer from severe water shortage, where the annual rate of cubic meters per person is less than 500. Every time there are more and more regions suffering from a chronic shortage of this vital resource.

»An insufficient amount of the precious fluid necessary to produce foodstuffs, the impaired development of industry, urban areas and tourism, and the emergence of health problems are some of the consequences that derive from water shortage».

So much for the TELAM wire service.

I have not mentioned other important facts, such as the ice that is melting down in Greenland and the Antarctic, the damages caused to the ozone layer and the ever higher titers of mercury found in many fish species which are part of the regular people's diet.

Other topics could be addressed, but in these few lines I simply intend to make some comments about the meeting held by President Bush with the chief executives of US automakers.

March 28, 2007
Fidel Castro Ruz

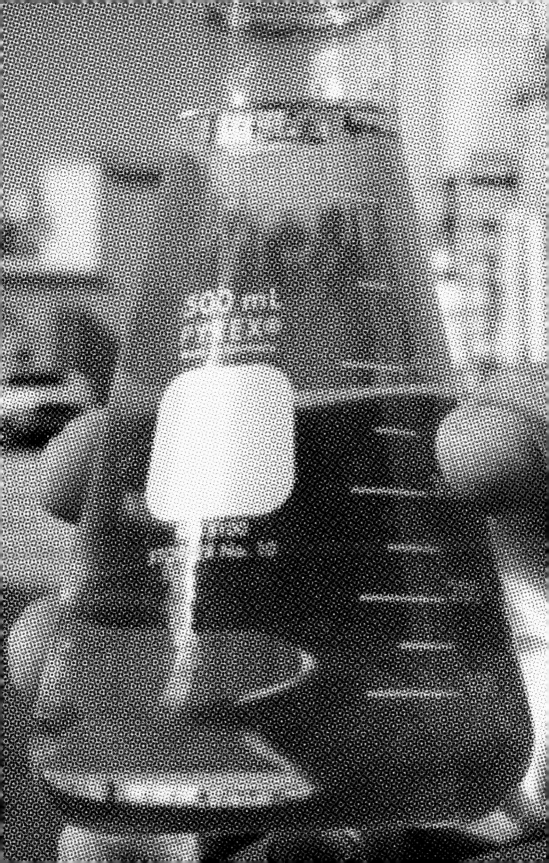

THE INTERNATIONALIZATION
OF GENOCIDE

The Camp David meeting has just come to an end. All of us followed the press conference offered by the presidents of the United States and Brazil attentively, as we did the news surrounding the meeting and the opinions voiced in this connection.

«Faced with demands related to customs duties and subsidies which protect and support US ethanol production, Bush did not make the slightest concession to his Brazilian guest at Camp David»

Faced with demands related to customs duties and subsidies which protect and support US ethanol production, Bush did not make the slightest concession to his Brazilian guest at Camp David.

President Lula attributed to this the rise in corn prices, which, according to his own statements, had gone up more than 85 percent.

Before these statements were made, *The Washington Post* had published an article by the Brazilian leader which expounded on the idea of transforming food into fuel.

It is not my intention to hurt Brazil or to meddle in the internal affairs of this great country. It was in effect in Rio de Janeiro, host of the United Nations Conference on Environment and Development, exactly 15 years ago, where I delivered a 7-minute speech vehemently denouncing the environ-

«Where are the more than 500 million tons of corn and other cereals which the United States, Europe and wealthy nations require to produce the gallons of ethanol that big companies in the United States and other countries demand in exchange for their voluminous investments going to be produced and who is going to supply them?»

mental dangers that menaced our species' survival. Bush Sr., then President of the United States, was present at that meeting and applauded my words out of courtesy; all other presidents there applauded, too.

No one at Camp David answered the fundamental question. Where are the more than 500 million tons of corn and other cereals which the United States, Europe and wealthy nations require to produce the gallons of ethanol that big companies in the United States and other countries demand in exchange for their voluminous investments going to be produced and who is going to supply them? Where are the soy, sunflower and rape seeds, whose essential oils these same, wealthy nations are to turn into fuel, going to be produced and who will produce them?

Some countries are food producers which export their surpluses. The balance of exporters and consumers had already become precarious before this and food prices had skyrocketed. In the interest of brevity, I shall limit myself to pointing out the following:

According to recent data, the five chief producers of corn, barley, sorghum, rye, millet and oat which Bush wants to transform into the raw material of ethanol production, supply the world market with 679 million tons of these products. Similarly, the five chief consumers, some of which also produce these grains, currently require 604 million annual tons of these products. The available surplus is less than 80 million tons of grain.

This colossal squandering of cereals destined to fuel production –and these estimates do not include data on oilseeds– shall serve to save rich countries less than 15 percent of the total annual consumption of their voracious automobiles.

At Camp David, Bush declared his intention of applying this formula around the world. This spells nothing other than the internationalization of genocide.

In his statements, published by *The Washington Post* on the eve of the Camp David meeting, the Brazilian president affirmed that less than one percent of Brazil's arable land was used to grow cane destined to ethanol production. This is nearly three times the land surface Cuba used when it produced nearly 10 million tons of sugar a year, before the crisis that befell the Soviet Union and the advent of climate changes.

Our country has been producing and exporting sugar for a longer time. First, on the basis of the work of slaves, whose numbers swelled to over 300 thousand in the first years of the 19th century and who turned the Spanish colony into the world's number one exporter. Nearly one hundred years later, at the beginning of the 20th century, when Cuba was a pseudo-republic which had been denied full independence by US interventionism, it was immigrants from the West Indies and illiterate Cubans alone who bore the burden of growing and harvesting sugarcane on the island. The scourge of our people was the off-season, inherent to the cyclical nature of the harvest. Sugarcane plantations were the property of

«This colossal squandering of cereals destined to fuel production (...) shall serve to save rich countries less than 15 percent of the total annual consumption of their voracious automobiles»

US companies or powerful Cuban-born landowners. Cuba, thus, has more experience than anyone as regards the social impact of this crop.

This past Sunday, April 1, the CNN televised the opinions of Brazilian experts who affirm that many lands destined to sugarcane have been purchased by wealthy Americans and Europeans.

As part of my reflections on the subject, published on March 29, I expounded on the impact climate change has had on Cuba and on other basic characteristics of our country's climate which contribute to this.

On our poor and anything but consumerist island, one would be unable to find enough workers to endure the rigors of the harvest and to care for the sugarcane plantations in the ever more intense heat, rains or droughts. When hurricanes lash the island, not even the best machines can harvest the bent-over and twisted canes. For centuries, the practice of burning sugarcane was unknown and no soil was compacted under the weight of complex machines and enormous trucks. Nitrogen, potassium and phosphate fertilizers, today extremely expensive, did not yet even exist, and the dry and wet months succeeded each other regularly. In modern agriculture, no high yields are possible without crop rotation methods.

On Sunday, April 1, the French Press Agency (AFP) published disquieting reports on the subject of climate change, which experts gathered by the United Nations already consider an inevitable phenomenon that will spell serious repercussions for the world in the coming decades.

«According to a UN report to be approved next week in Brussels, climate change will have a significant impact on the American continent, generating more violent storms and heat

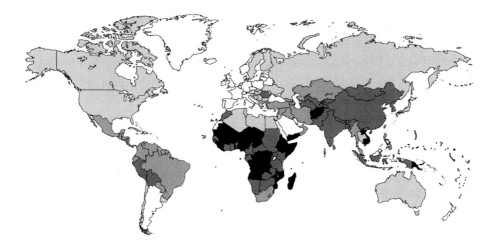

ACCESS TO WATER AND SANITATION SERVICES

■ Extreme risk
(less than 50 %)

▨ Low risk
(more than 90 %)

▨ High risk
(50-74 %)

☐ No data

▨ Moderate risk
(75-90 %)

Source: United Nations
www.worldwaterday.net

THE WORLD WATER CRISIS

In 2005, one third of the world's population lived in countries suffering water shortages. This situation, it is feared, will now come to affect two thirds of this population.

In the world, there are 1.1 billion people who lack drinkable water and 2.4 billion who have no access to sanitation services (sewer systems, waste treatment, latrines, etc.). This has a dramatic impact upon the lives of many people, revealing the link between poverty, water availability and health.

In a number of South countries, such as Sub-Saharan Africa, people survive on less than 10 litres of water a day, when the UN estimates that 40 litres is the minimum requirement for a healty life. The main illnesses caused by the absence of water and sanitation services are: gastroenteritis, parasitosis, cholera, cutaneous infections, dehydration and malaria. These illnesses cause the deaths of 2,500 people every day. Children under five and pregnant women are the most vulnerable groups.

«In Latin America, global warming is already melting glaciers in the Andes and threatening the Amazon forest, whose perimeter may slowly be turned into a savanna»

waves and causing droughts, the extinction of some species and even hunger in Latin America».

The AFP report indicates that the Intergovernmental Panel on Climate Change (IPCC) forewarned that at the end of this century, every hemisphere will endure water-related problems and, if governments take no measures in this connection, rising temperatures could increase the risks of mortality, contamination, natural catastrophes and infectious diseases.

«In Latin America, global warming is already melting glaciers in the Andes and threatening the Amazon forest, whose perimeter may slowly be turned into a savanna, the cable goes on to report.

»Because a great part of its population lives near the coast, the United States is also vulnerable to extreme natural phenomena, as hurricane Katrina demonstrated in 2005.

»According to AFP, this is the second of three IPCC reports which began to be published last February, following an initial scientific forecast which established the certainty of climate change.

»This second 1400-page report which analyzes climate change in different sectors and regions, of which AFP has obtained a copy, considers that, even if radical measures to reduce carbon dioxide emissions that pollute the atmosphere are taken, the rise in temperatures around the planet in the coming decades is already unavoidable» –concludes the French Press Agency.

As was to be expected, at the Camp David meeting, Dan Fisk, National Security advisor for the region, declared that

28

SEA ICE COVER

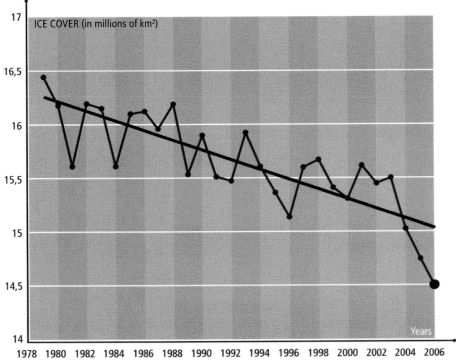

ICE COVER (in millions of km²)

Years

«Cuba's infant mortality rate is lower than the United States'. All citizens –this is beyond question– enjoy free medical services. Everyone has access to education and no one is denieemployment, in spite of nearly half a century of economic blockade»

«in the discussion on regional issues, [I expect] Cuba to come up (...) if there's anyone that knows how to create star\ation, it's Fidel Castro. He also knows how not to do ethanol».

As I find myself obliged to respond to this gentleman, it is my duty to remind him that Cuba's infant mortality rate is lower than the United States'. All citizens –this is beyond question– enjoy free medical services. Everyone has access to education and no one is denied employment, in spite of nearly half a century of economic blockade and the attempts of US governments to starve and economically asphyxiate the people of Cuba.

China would never devote a single ton of cereals or leguminous plants to the production of ethanol, and it is an economically prosperous nation which is breaking growth records, where all citizens earn the income they need to purchase essential consumer items, despite the fact that 48 percent of its population, which exceeds 1.3 billion, works in agriculture. On the contrary, it has set out to reduce energy consumption considerably by shutting down thousands of factories which consume unacceptable amounts of electricity and hydrocarbons. It imports many of the food products mentioned above from far-off corners of the world, transporting these over thousands of miles.

Scores of countries do not produce hydrocarbons and are unable to produce corn and other grains or oilseeds, for they do not even have enough water to meet their most basic needs.

At a meeting on ethanol production held in Buenos Aires by the Argentine Oil Industry Chamber and Cereals Exporters Association, Loek Boonekamp, the Dutch head of the Organization for Economic Cooperation and Development (OECD) commercial and marketing division, told the press that governments are very much enthused about this process but that they should objectively consider whether ethanol ought to be given such resolute support.

According to Boonekamp, the United States is the only country where ethanol can be profitable and, without subsidies, no other country can make it viable.

According to the report, Boonekamp insists that ethanol is not manna from Heaven and that we should not blindly commit to developing this process.

«Today, developed countries are pushing to have fossil fuels mixed with biofuels at around five percent and this is already affecting agricultural prices. If this figure went up to 10 percent, 30 percent of the United States' cultivated surface and 50 percent of Europe's would be required. That is the reason Boonekamp asks himself whether the process is sustainable, as an increase in the demand for crops destined to ethanol production would generate higher and less stable prices».

Protectionist measures are today at 54 cents per gallon and real subsidies reach far higher figures.

Applying the simple arithmetic we learned in high school, we could show how, by simply replacing incandescent bulbs with fluorescent ones, as I explained in my previous reflections, millions and millions of dollars in investment and

«Scores of countries do not produce hydrocarbons and are unable to produce corn and other grains or oilseeds, for they do not even have enough water to meet their most basic needs»

«By simply replacing incandescent bulbs with fluorescent ones, millions and millions of dollars in investment and energy could be saved, without the need to use a single acre of farming land»

energy could be saved, without the need to use a single acre of farming land.

In the meantime, we are receiving news from Washington, through the AP, reporting:

«That the mysterious disappearance of millions of bees throughout the United States has edged beekeepers to the brink of a nervous breakdown and is even cause for concern in Congress, which will discuss this Thursday the critical situation facing this insect, essential to the agricultural sector. According to the report, the first disquieting signs of this enigma became evident shortly after Christmas in the state of Florida, when beekeepers discovered that their bees had vanished without a trace. Since then, the syndrome which experts have christened as Colony Collapse Disorder (CCD) has reduced the country's swarms by 25 percent.

»Daniel Weaver, president of the US Beekeepers Association, stated that more than half a million colonies, each with a population of nearly 50 thousand bees, had been lost. He added that the syndrome has struck 30 of the country's 50 states. What is curious about the phenomenon is that, in many cases, the mortal remains of the bees are not found.

»According to a study conducted by Cornell University, these industrious insects pollinate crops valued at anywhere from 12 to 14 billion dollars.

»Scientists are entertaining all kinds of hypotheses, including the theory that a pesticide may have caused the bees' neurological damage and altered their sense of orientation. Others lay the blame on the drought and even mobile phone waves, but, what's certain is that no one knows exactly what has unleashed this syndrome».

The worst may be yet to come: a new war aimed at securing gas and oil supplies that can take humanity to the brink of total annihilation.

Invoking intelligence sources, Russian newspapers have reported that a war on Iran has been in the works for over three years now, since the day the government of the United States resolved to occupy Iraq completely, unleashing a seemingly endless and despicable civil war.

All the while, the government of the United States devotes hundreds of billions to the development of highly sophisticated technologies, as those which employ micro-electronic systems or new nuclear weapons which can strike their targets an hour following the order to attack.

The United States brazenly turns a deaf ear to world public opinion, which is against all kinds of nuclear weapons.

Razing all of Iran's factories to the ground is a relatively easy task, from the technical point of view, for a powerful country like the United States. The difficult task may come later, if a new war were to be unleashed against another Muslim faith which deserves our utmost respect, as do all other religions of the Near, Middle or Far East, predating or post-dating Christianity.

The arrest of English soldiers at Iran's territorial waters recalls the nearly identical act of provocation of the so-called «Brothers to the Rescue» who, ignoring President Clinton's orders advanced over our country's territorial waters. Cuba's absolutely legitimate

«The worst may be yet to come: a new war aimed at securing gas and oil supplies that can take humanity to the brink of total annihilation» and defensive action gave the United States a pretext to promulgate the well-renowned Helms-Burton Act, which encroaches upon the sovereignty of other nations besides Cuba. The powerful media have consigned that episode to oblivion. No few people attribute the price of oil, at nearly 70 dollars a gallon as of Monday, to fears of a possible invasion of Iran.

Where shall poor Third World countries find the basic resources needed to survive?

I am not exaggerating or using overblown language. I am confining myself to the facts.

As can be seen, the polyhedron has many dark faces.

April 3, 2007
Fidel Castro Ruz

A BRUTAL REPLY

INJUSTICE TREMBLES

HENCHMEN OF DEATH

HENCHMEN OF DEATH
JUSTICE
EMBLES

George W. Bush is undoubtedly the most genuine representative of a system of terror forced on the world by the technological, economic and political superiority of the most powerful country known to this planet. For this reason, we share the tragedy of the American people and their ethical values. The instructions for the verdict issued by Judge Kathleen Cardone, of the El Paso Federal Court last Friday, granting Luis Posada Carriles freedom on bail, could only have come from the White House.

«The reply is brutal. The government of the United States and its most representative institutions had already decided to release the monster»

It was President Bush himself who ignored at all times the criminal and terrorist nature of the defendant who was protected with a simple accusation of immigration violation leveled at him. The reply is brutal. The government of the United States and its most representative institutions had already decided to release the monster.

The backgrounds are well-known and reach far back. The people who trained him and ordered him to destroy a Cuban passenger plane in midair, with 73 athletes, students and other Cuban and foreign travelers on board, together with

«Even though Bush's decision was to be expected, it is certainly no less humiliating for our people»

its dedicated crew; those who bought his freedom while the terrorist was held in prison in Venezuela, so that he could supply and practically conduct a dirty war against the people of Nicaragua, resulting in the loss of thousands of lives and the devastation of a country for decades to come; those who empowered him to smuggle with drugs and weapons making a mockery of the laws of Congress; those who collaborated with him to create the terrible Operation Condor and to internationalize terror; the same who brought torture, death and often the physical disappearance of hundreds of thousands of Latin Americans, could not possibly act any different.

Even though Bush's decision was to be expected, it is certainly no less humiliating for our people. Thanks to the revelations of *"Por Esto!"* a Mexican publication from the state of Quintana Roo later complemented by our own sources, Cuba knew with absolute precision how Posada Carriles entered from Central America, via Cancun, to the Isla Mujeres departing from there on board the Santrina, after the ship was inspected by the Mexican federal authorities, heading with other terrorists straight to Miami.

Denounced and publicly challenged with exact information on the matter, since April 11, 2005, it took the government of that country more than a month to arrest the terrorist, and a year and two months to admit that Luis Posada Carriles had entered through the Florida coast illegally on board the Santrina, a presumed school-ship licensed in the United States.

Not a single word is said of his countless victims, of the bombs he set off in tourist facilities in recent years, of his dozens of plans financed by the government of the United States to physically eliminate me.

It was not enough for Bush to offend the name of Cuba by installing a horrible torture center similar to Abu Ghraib on the territory illegally occupied in Guantánamo, horrifying the world with this procedure. The cruel actions of his predecessors seemed not enough for him. It was not enough to force a poor and underdeveloped country like Cuba to spend 100 billion dollars. To accuse Posada Carriles was tantamount to accusing himself.

Throughout almost half a century, everything was fair game against our small island lying 90 miles away from its coast, wanting to be independent. Florida saw the installation of the largest station for intelligence and subversion that ever existed on this planet.

It was not enough to send a mercenary invasion on the Bay of Pigs, costing us 176 dead and more than 300 wounded at a time when the few medical specialists they left us had no experience treating war wounds.

Earlier still, the French ship *La Coubre* carrying Belgian weapons and grenades for Cuba had exploded on the docks of Havana Harbor. The two well synchronized explosions caused the deaths of more than 100 workers and wounded others as many of them took part in the rescue attempts.

It was not enough to have the Missile Crisis of 1962, which brought the world to the brink of an all-consuming thermonuclear war, at a time when there were bombs 50 times more powerful than the ones dropped on Hiroshima and Nagasaki.

«Not a single word is said of his countless victims, of the bombs he set off in tourist facilities in recent years, of his dozens of plans financed by the government of the United States to physically eliminate me»

«The enormous injustice of keeping five heroic patriots imprisoned for supplying information about terrorist activities; they were condemned in a fraudulent manner to sentences that include two life sentences and they stoically withstand cruel mistreatment, each of them in a different prison»

It was not enough to introduce in our country viruses, bacteria and fungi to attack plantations and flocks; and incredible as it may seem, to attack human beings. Some of these pathogens came out of American laboratories and were brought to Cuba by well-known terrorists in the service of the United States government.

Add to all this the enormous injustice of keeping five heroic patriots imprisoned for supplying information about terrorist activities; they were condemned in a fraudulent manner to sentences that include two life sentences and they stoically withstand cruel mistreatment, each of them in a different prison.

Time and again the Cuban people have fearlessly faced the threat of death. They have demonstrated that with intelligence, using appropriate tactics and strategies, and especially preserving unity around their political and social vanguard, there can be no force on this Earth capable of defeating them.

I think that the coming May Day celebration would be the ideal day for our people, –using the minimum of fuel and transportation– to show their feelings to the workers and the poor of the world.

Fidel Castro Ruz
April 10, 2007

IT IS IMPERATIVE TO IMMEDIATELY
HAVE AN ENERGY REVOLUTION

hold nothing against Brazil, even though to more than a few Brazilians continuously bombarded with the most diverse arguments, which can be confusing even for people who have traditionally been

«Keep silent would be to opt between the idea of a world tragedy and a presumed benefit for the people of that great nation»

friendly to Cuba, we might sound callous and careless about hurting that country's net income of hard currency. However, for me to keep silent would be to opt between the idea of a world tragedy and a presumed benefit for the people of that great nation.

I do not blame Lula and the Brazilians for the objective laws which have governed the history of our species. Only seven thousand years have passed since the human being has left his tangible mark on what has come to be a civilization immensely rich in culture and technical knowledge. Advances have not been achieved at the same time or in the same geographical latitudes. It can be said that due to the apparent enormity of our planet, quite often the existence of one or another civilization was unknown. Never in thousands of years had the human being lived in cities with twenty million inhabitants such as Sao Paulo or Mexico City, or in urban communities

«Today, the world has tens of thousands of nuclear bombs that are fifty times as powerful, with carriers that are several times faster than the speed of sound and having absolute precision; our sophisticated species could destroy itself with them»

such as Paris, Madrid, Berlin and others who see trains speeding by on rails and air cushions, at speeds of more than 250 miles an hour.

At the time of Christopher Columbus, barely 500 years ago, some of these cities did not exist or they had populations that did not exceed several tens of thousands. Nobody used one single kilowatt to light its home. Possibly, the population of the world then was not more than 500 million. We know that in 1830, world population reached the first billion mark, one hundred and thirty years later it multiplied by three, and forty-six years later the total number of inhabitants on the planet had grown to 6.5 billion; the immense majority of these were poor, having to share their food with domestic animals and from now on with biofuels.

Humanity did not then have all the advances in computers and means of communication that we have today, even though the first atomic bombs had already been detonated over two large human communities, in a brutal act of terrorism against a defenseless civilian population, for reasons that were strictly political.

Today, the world has tens of thousands of nuclear bombs that are fifty times as powerful, with carriers that are several times faster than the speed of sound and having absolute precision; our sophisticated species could destroy itself with them. At the end of World War II, fought by the peoples against fascism, a new power emerged that took over the

44

world and imposed the absolutist and cruel order under which we live today.

Before Bush's trip to Brazil, the leader of the empire decided that corn and other foodstuffs would be suitable raw material for the production of biofuels. For his part, Lula stated that Brazil could supply as much biofuel as necessary from sugar cane; he saw in this formula a possibility for the future of the Third World, and the only problem left to solve would be to improve the living conditions of the sugarcane workers. He was well aware –and he said it– that the United States should in turn lift the custom tariffs and the subsidies affecting ethanol exports to that country.

Bush replied that custom tariffs and subsidies to the growers were untouchable in a country such as the United States, which is the first world producer of ethanol from corn.

The large American transnationals, which produce this biofuel investing tens of billions of dollars at an accelerated pace, had demanded from the imperial leader the distribution in the American market of no less than thirty-five billion (35,000,000,000) gallons of this fuel every year. The combination of protective tariffs and real subsidies would raise that figure to almost one hundred billion dollars each year.

Insatiable in its demand, the empire had flung into the world the slogan of producing biofuels in order to liberate the United States, the world's supreme energy consumer, from all external dependency on hydrocarbons.

History shows that sugar as a single crop was closely associated with the enslaving of Africans, forcibly uprooted from their natural communities, and brought to Cuba, Haiti and other Caribbean islands. In Brazil, the exact same thing happened in the growing of sugar cane.

«The empire had flung into the world the slogan of producing biofuels in order to liberate the United States, the world's supreme energy consumer, from all external dependency on hydrocarbons»

Today, in that country, almost 80% of sugar cane is cut by hand. Sources and studies made by Brazilian researchers affirm that a sugarcane cutter, a piecework laborer, must produce no less than twelve tons in order to meet basic needs. This worker needs to perform 36,630 flexing movements with his legs, make small trips 800 times carrying 15 kilos of cane in his arms and walk 8,800 meters in his chores. He loses an average of 8 liters of water every day. Only by burning cane can this productivity per man be achieved. Cane cut by hand or by machines is usually burned to protect people from nasty bites and especially to increase productivity. Even though the established norm for a working day is from 8 in the morning until 5 in the afternoon, this type of piece-work cane cutting tends to go on for a 12 hour working day. The temperature will at times rise to 45 degrees centigrade by noon.

I have cut cane myself more than once as a moral duty, as have many other comrade leaders of the country. I remember August of 1969. I chose a place close to the capital. I moved there very early every day. It was not burned cane but green cane, an early variety and high in agricultural and industrial yield. I would cut for four hours nonstop. Somebody else would be sharpening the machete. I consistently produced a minimum of 3.4 tons per day. Then I would shower, calmly have some lunch and take a break in a place nearby. I earned several coupons in the famous harvest of 1970. I had just turned 43 then. The rest of the time, until bedtime, I worked at my revolutionary duties. I stopped my personal efforts after I wounded my left foot. The sharpened machete had sliced through my protective boot. The national goal was 10 million tons of sugar and approximately 4 million tons of molasses as by-product. We never reached that goal, although we came close.

The USSR had not disappeared; that seemed impossible. The Special Period, which took us to a struggle for survival and to economic inequalities with their inherent elements of corruption, had not yet begun. Imperialism believed that the time had come to finish off the Revolution. It is also fair to recognize that during years of bonanza we wasted resources and our idealism ran high along with the dreams accompanying our heroic process.

The great agricultural yields of the United States were achieved by rotating the gramineae (corn, wheat, oat, millet and other similar grains) with the legumes (soy, alfalfa, beans, etc.). These contribute nitrogen and organic material to the soil. The corn crop yield in the United States in 2005, according to FAO (Food and Agriculture Organization of the United Nations) data was 9.3 tons per hectare.

In Brazil they only obtain 3 tons of this same grain in the same area. The total production registered by this sister nation that year was thirty-four million six hundred thousand tons, consumed internally as food. It cannot contribute corn to the world market.

The prices for this grain, the staple diet in numerous countries of the region, have almost doubled. What will happen when hundreds of millions of

«The corn crop yield in the United States in 2005, according to FAO (Food and Agriculture Organization of the United Nations) data was 9.3 tons per hectare. In Brazil they only obtain 3 tons of this same grain in the same area»

«What will happen when hundreds of millions of tons of corn are redirected towards the production of biofuel?»

tons of corn are redirected towards the production of biofuel? And I rather not mention the amounts of wheat, millet, oat, barley, sorghum and other cereals that industrialized countries will use as a source of fuel for its engines.

Add to this that it is very difficult for Brazil to rotate corn and legumes. Of the Brazilian states traditionally producing corn, eight are responsible for ninety percent of production: Paraná, Minas Gerais, Sao Paulo, Goiás, Mato Grosso, Rio Grande do Sul, Santa Catarina and Mato Grosso do Sul. On the other hand, 60% of sugarcane production, a grain that cannot be rotated with other crops, takes place in the state of Sao Paulo, and also in the states of Paraná, Pernambuco and Alagoas.

The engines of tractors, harvesters and the heavy machinery required to mechanize the harvest would use growing amounts of hydrocarbons. The increase of mechanization would not help in the prevention of global warming, something which has been proven by experts who have measured annual temperatures for the last 150 years.

Brazil does produce an excellent food that is especially rich in protein: soy, fifty million one hundred and fifteen thousand (50,115,000) tons. It consumes almost 23 million tons and exports twenty-seven million three hundred thousand (27,300,000). Is it perhaps that a large part of this soy will be converted to biofuel?

As it is, the producers of beef cattle are beginning to complain that grazing land is being transformed into sugarcane fields.

The former Agriculture Minister of Brazil, Roberto Rodrigues, an important advocate for the current government position, –and today a co-president of the Inter American Ethanol Commission created in 2006 following an agreement with the state of Florida and the Inter American Development Bank (IDB) to promote the use of biofuel on the American continent– declared that the program to mechanize the sugarcane harvest does not create more jobs, but on the contrary it would produce a surplus of non-qualified manpower.

We know that the poorest workers from various states are the ones who gravitate towards cane cutting out of necessity. Sometimes, they must spend many months away from their families. That is what happened in Cuba until the triumph of the Revolution, when the cutting and hauling of sugarcane was done by hand, and mechanized cultivation or transportation hardly existed. With the demise of the brutal system forced on our society the cane-cutters, massively taught to read and write, abandoned their wanderings in a few years and it became necessary to replace them with hundreds of thousands of voluntary workers.

Add to this the latest report by the United Nations about climate change, affirming what would happen in South America with the water from the glaciers and the Amazon water basin as the temperature of the atmosphere continue to rise.

Nothing could prevent American and European capital from funding the production of biofuels. They could

«Nothing could prevent American and European capital from funding the production of biofuels. They could even send the funds as gifts to Brazil and Latin America. The United States, Europe and the other industrialized countries would save more than one hundred and forty billion dollars each year, without having to worry about the consequences for the climate and the hunger»

GLOBAL ETHANOL PRODUCTION (IN MILLION OF LITRES)

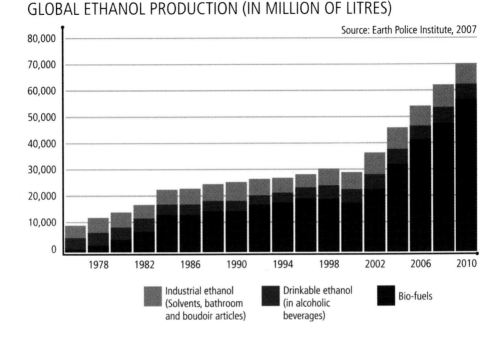

Source: Earth Police Institute, 2007

Industrial ethanol (Solvents, bathroom and boudoir articles) | Drinkable ethanol (in alcoholic beverages) | Bio-fuels

even send the funds as gifts to Brazil and Latin America. The United States, Europe and the other industrialized countries would save more than one hundred and forty billion dollars each year, without having to worry about the consequences for the climate and the hunger which would affect the countries of the Third World in the first place. They would always be left with enough money for biofuels and to acquire the little food available on the world market at any price.

It is imperative to immediately have an energy revolution that consists not only in replacing all the incandescent light bulbs, but also in massively recycling all domestic, commercial, industrial, transport and socially used electric appliances that require two and three times more energy with their previous technologies.

It hurts to think that 10 billion tons of fossil fuel are consumed every year. This means that each year we waste what it took nature a million years to create. National industries are faced with enormous challenges, including the reduction of unemployment. Thus we could gain a bit of time.

Another risk of a different nature facing the world is an economic recession in the United States. In the past few days, the dollar has broken records at losing value. On the other hand, every country has most of its reserves in convertible currencies precisely in this paper currency and in American bonds.

Tomorrow, May Day is a good day to bring these reflections to the workers and to all the poor people of the world. At the same time we should protest against something incredible and humiliating that has just occurred: the liberation of a terrorist monster, exactly when we are celebrating the 46th Anniversary of the Revolutionary Victory at Bay of Pigs.

Prison for the assassin!
Freedom for the Five Cuban Heroes!

Fidel Castro Ruz
April 30, 2007
6:34 p.m.

THE TRAGEDY THREATENING OUR SPECIES

I cannot speak as an econo- «Every evil idea must be
mist or a scientist. I simply submitted to devastating
speak as a politician who criticism, avoiding
wishes to unravel the econo- any concession»
mists' and scientists' argu-
ments one way or another. I also try to sense the motivations
of each one of those who make statements on these matters.
Just twenty-two years ago, here in Havana, we had a great
number of meetings with political, union, peasant and student leaders invited to our country as representatives of these
sectors. They all agreed that the most important problem at
that time was the enormous foreign debt accumulated by the
nations of Latin America in 1985. That debt amounted to 350
billion dollars. The dollar then had a higher purchasing power
than it does today.

A copy of the outcome of those meetings was sent to all
the world governments, of course with some exceptions, because it might have seemed insulting. At that time, the petro-
dollars had flooded the market and the large transnational
banks were virtually demanding that the countries accept high
loans. Needless to say, the people responsible for the economy
had taken on those commitments without consulting anybody.
That period coincided with the presence of the most repressive

«Today, in the Latin American region, the difference between the most favored population and the one with the lowest income is the greatest in the world»

and bloody governments this continent has ever suffered, installed by imperialism. Large sums were spent on weapons, luxuries and consumer goods. The subsequent debt grew to 800 billion dollars while today's catastrophic dangers were being hatched, the dangers that weigh upon a population that doubled in just two decades and along with it, the number of those condemned to a life of extreme poverty. Today, in the Latin American region, the difference between the most favored population and the one with the lowest income is the greatest in the world.

Many years before the subjects of today's debates were center stage, the struggles of the Third World focused on equally agonizing problems like the unequal exchange. Year after year it was discovered that the price of the industrialized nations' exports, usually manufactured with our raw materials, would unilaterally grow while our basic exports remained unchanged. The price of coffee and cacao, just to mention two examples, was approximately 2,000 dollars a ton. A cup of coffee or a chocolate milkshake could be bought in cities like New York for a few cents; today, these cost several dollars, perhaps 30 or 40 times what they cost back then. Today, the purchase of a tractor, a truck or medical equipment require several times the volume of products that was needed to import them back then; jute, henequen and other Third World produced fibers that were substituted by synthetic ones succumbed to the same fate. In the meantime, tanned hides, rubber and natural fibers used in many textiles were being replaced by synthetic materials derived from the sophisticated petrochemical industry while sugar prices hit rock bottom, crushed by the large subsidies granted by the industrialized countries to their agricultural sector.

The former colonies or neocolonies that had been promised a glowing future after World War II had not yet awakened from the Bretton Woods dream. From top to bottom, the system had been designed for exploitation and plundering.

When consciousness was beginning to be roused, the other extremely adverse factors had not yet surfaced, such as the undreamed-of squandering of energy that industrialized countries had fallen prey to. They were paying less than two dollars a barrel of oil. The source of fuel, with the exception of the United States where it was very abundant, was basically in Third World countries, chiefly in the Middle East but also in Mexico, Venezuela, and later in Africa. But not all of the countries that by virtue of yet another white lie classified as «developing countries» were oil producers, since 82 of them are among the poorest and as a rule they must import oil. A terrible situation awaits them if foodstuffs are to be transformed into biofuels or agrifuels, as the peasant and native movements in our region prefer to call them.

Thirty years ago, the idea of global warming hanging over our species' life like a sword of Damocles was not even known by the immense majority of the inhabitants of our planet; even today there is great ignorance and confu-

«Thirty years ago, the idea of global warming hanging over our species' life like a sword of Damocles was not even known by the immense majority of the inhabitants of our planet; even today there is great ignorance and confusion about these issues»

sion about these issues. If we listen to the spokesmen of the transnationals and their media, we are living in the best of all possible worlds: an economy ruled by the market, plus transnational capital, plus sophisticated technology equals a constant growth of productivity, higher GDP, higher living standards and every dream of the human species come true; the state should not interfere with anything, it should not even exist, other than as an instrument of the large financial capital.

But reality is hard-headed. Germany, one of the most highly industrialized countries in the world, loses sleep over its 10 percent unemployment. The toughest and least attractive jobs are taken by immigrants who, desperate in their growing poverty, break into industrialized Europe through any possible chink. Apparently, nobody is taking note of the number of inhabitants on our planet, growing precisely in the undeveloped countries.

More than 700 representatives of social organizations have just been meeting in Havana to discuss various issues raised in this reflection. Many of them set out their points of view and left indelible impressions on us. There is plenty of material to reflect upon as well as new events happening every day.

Even now, as a consequence of liberating a terrorist monster, two young men, who were fulfilling their legal duty in the Active Military Service, anxious to taste consumerism in the United States, hijacked a bus, crashed through one of the doors of the domestic flights terminal at the airport, drove up to a civilian aircraft and got on board with their hostages, demanding to be taken to the United States. A few days earlier, they had killed a soldier, who was standing guard, to steal two automatic weapons, and in the plane they fired four shots that killed a brave officer who, unarmed and held hos-

ASIA'S TIDAL WAVE: TWO YEARS LATER

Over two years after the tidal wave which shook the Indian Ocean on December 26ᵗʰ, 2004, 229,866 people are believed to have perished or disappeared. In spite of the US $ 3 billion donated to the victims, many of the two million people who were left homeless or were displaced by the disaster still do not have proper homes to live in.

Source: UN Office of the Special Envoy for Tsunami Recovery, 2007

ESTIMATED NUMBER OF VICTIMS

Indonesia: 130, 736 dead; 37,000 disappeared	**Malaysia:** 69 dead; 6 disappeared
Sri Lanka: 35, 322 dead	**Myanmar:** 61 dead
India: 12,405 dead; 5, 640 disappeared	**Tanzania:** 13 dead
Thailand: 8, 212 dead	**Bangladesh:** 2 dead
Somalia: 78 dead; 211 disappeared	**Seychelles:** 2 dead
Maldives: 82 dead; 26 disappeared	**Kenya:** 1 dead

«The apocalyptic head of the empire declared more than five years ago that the United States armed forces had to be on the ready to make pre-emptive attacks on 60 or more countries in the world; nothing less than one third of the international community. Apparently, he is not satisfied with the death, the torture and the uprooting of millions of people to seize their natural resources and the product of their labors»

tage in the bus, had attempted to prevent the plane's hijacking. The impunity and the material gains that have rewarded any violent action against Cuba during the last half-century encourage such events. It had been many months since we had such an incident. All it needed was setting a notorious terrorist free and once again death come calling at our door. The perpetrators have not gone on trial yet because, in the course of events, both were wounded; one of them was shot by the other as he fired inside the plane, while they were struggling with the heroic army officer. Now, many people abroad are waiting for the reaction of our Courts and of the Council of State, while our people here are deeply outraged with these events. We really need a large dose of calmness and sangfroid to confront these problems.

The apocalyptic head of the empire declared more than five years ago that the United States armed forces had to be on the ready to make pre-emptive attacks on 60 or more countries in the world; nothing less than one third of the international community. Apparently, he is not satisfied with the death, the torture and the uprooting of millions of people to seize their natural resources and the product of their labors.

Meanwhile, the impressive international meeting that just concluded in Havana reaffirmed my personal conviction: every evil idea must be submitted to devastating criticism, avoiding any concession.

Fidel Castro Ruz
May 7, 2007
5:42 p.m.

THE DEBATE HEATS UP

Atilio Borón, a prestigious leftist intellectual who until recently headed the Latin American Council of Social Sciences (CLACSO), wrote an article

«Capitalism is preparing to perpetrate a massive euthanasia on the poor, and particularly on the poor of the South»

for the 6th Hemispheric Meeting of Struggle against the FTAs and for the Integration of Peoples which just wrapped up in Havana; he was kind enough to send it to me along with a letter.

The gist of what he wrote I have summarized using exact quotes of paragraphs and phrases in his article; it reads as follows:

Pre-capitalist societies already knew about oil which surfaced in shallow deposits and they used for non-commercial purposes, such as waterproofing the wooden hulls of ships or in textile products, or for torches. Its original name was 'petroleum' or stone-oil.

By the end of the 19th century –after the discovery of large oilfields in Pennsylvania, United States, and the technological developments propelled by the massive use of the internal combustion engine– oil became the energy paradigm of the 20th century.

«Foodstuffs are transformed into fuels to make viable the irrationality of a civilization that, to sustain the wealth and privilege of a few, is brutally assaulting the environment»

Energy is conceived of as just merchandise. Like Marx warned us, this is not due to the perversity or callousness of some individual capitalist or another, but rather the consequence of the logic of the accumulation process, which is prone to the ceaseless «mercantilism» that touches on all components of social life, both material and symbolic. The mercantilist process did not stop with the human being, but simultaneously extended to nature. The land and its products, the rivers and the mountains, the jungles and the forests became the target of its irrepressible pillage. Foodstuffs, of course, could not escape this hellish dynamic. Capitalism turns everything that crosses its path into merchandise.

Foodstuffs are transformed into fuels to make viable the irrationality of a civilization that, to sustain the wealth and privilege of a few, is brutally assaulting the environment and the ecologic conditions which made it possible for life to appear on Earth.

Transforming food into fuels is a monstrosity.

Capitalism is preparing to perpetrate a massive euthanasia on the poor, and particularly on the poor of the South, since it is there that the greatest reserves of the Earth's biomass required to produce biofuels are found. Regardless of numerous official statements assuring that this is not a choice between food and fuel, reality shows that this, and no other, is exactly the alternative: either the land is used to produce food or to produce biofuels.

The main lessons taught us by FAO data on the subject of agricultural land and the consumption of fertilizers are the following:

- Agricultural land per capita in developed capitalism almost doubles that existing in the underdeveloped periphery: 3.26 acres per person in the North as opposed to 1.6 in the South; this is explained by the simple fact that close to 80 percent of the world population live in the underdeveloped periphery.
- Brazil has slightly more agricultural land per capita than the developed countries. It becomes clear that this nation will have to assign huge tracts of its enormous land surface to meet the demands of the new energy paradigm.
- China and India have 1.05 and 0.43 acres per person respectively.
- The small nations of the Antilles, with their traditional one-crop agriculture, that is sugarcane, demonstrate eloquently its erosive effects exemplified by the extraordinary rate of consumption of fertilizers per acre needed to support this production. If in the peripheral countries the average figure is 109 kilograms of fertilizer per hectare (as opposed to 84 in developed countries), in Barbados the figure is 187.5, in Dominica 600, en Guadeloupe 1,016, in St. Lucia 1,325 and in Martinique 1,609. The use of fertilizers is tantamount to intensive oil consumption, and so the much touted advantage of agrifuels to reduce the consumption of hydrocarbons seems more an illusion than a reality.

The total agricultural land of the European Union is barely sufficient to cover 30 percent of their current needs for fuel but not their future needs that will probably be greater. In the United States, the satisfaction of their current demand for fossil fuels would require the use of 121 percent of all their agricultural land for agrifuels.

«Transforming food into fuels is a monstrosity»

«In the United States, the satisfaction of their current demand for fossil fuels would require the use of 121 percent of all their agricultural land for agrifuels»

Consequently, the supply of agrifuels will have to come from the South, from capitalism's poor and neocolonial periphery. Mathematics does not lie: neither the United States nor the European Union have available land to support an increase in food production and an expansion of the production of agrifuels at the same time.

Deforestation of the planet would increase the land surface suitable for agriculture (but only for a while). Therefore this would be only for a few decades, at the most. These lands would then suffer desertification and the situation would be worse than ever, aggravating even further the dilemma pitting the production of food against that of ethanol or biodiesel.

The struggle against hunger –and there are some 2 billion people who suffer from hunger in the world– will be seriously impaired by the expansion of land taken over by agrifuel crops. Countries where hunger is a universal scourge will bear witness to the rapid transformation of agriculture that would feed the insatiable demand for fuels needed by a civilization based on their irrational use. The only result possible is an increase in the cost of food and thus, the worsening of the social situation in the South countries.

Moreover, the world population grows 76 million people every year who will obviously demand food that will be steadily more expensive and farther out of their reach.

In *The Globalist Perspective*, Lester Brown predicted less than a year ago that automobiles would absorb the largest part of the increase in world grain production in 2006. Of the

DEFORESTATION IN THE AMAZON

Annual loss of jungle cover estimate in square
kilometers (miles), calculated from data provided
by the Brazilian goverment.

Source: National Institute for Spatial Research, Brazil

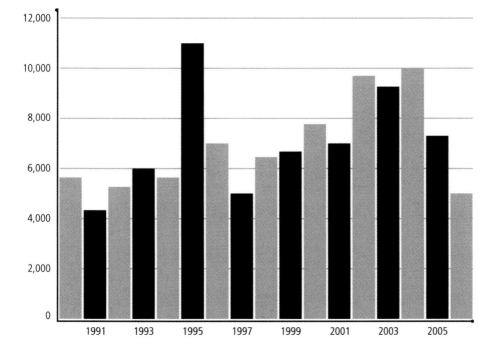

«The world population grows 76 million people every year who will obviously demand food that will be steadily more expensive and farther out of their reach»

20 million tons added to those existing in 2005, 14 million were used in the production of fuels, and only 6 million tons were used to satisfy the needs of the hungry. This author affirms that the world appetite for automobile fuel is insatiable. Brown concluded by saying that a scenario is being prepared where a head-on confrontation will take place between the 800 million prosperous car owners and the food consumers.

The devastating impact of increased food prices, which will inexorably happen as the land is used either for food or for fuel, was demonstrated in the work of C. Ford Runge and Benjamin Senauer, two distinguished professors from the University of Minnesota, in an article published in the English language edition of the *Foreign Affairs* magazine whose title says it all: «How Biofuels Could Starve the Poor». The authors claim that in the United States the growth of the agrifuel industry has given rise to increases not only in the price of corn, oleaginous seeds and other grains, but also in the prices of apparently unrelated crops and products. The use of land to grow corn which will feed the fauces of ethanol is reducing the area for other crops. The food processors using crops such as peas and young corn have been forced to pay higher prices in order to ensure their supplies. This is a cost that will eventually be passed on to the consumer. The increase in food prices is also hitting the livestock and poultry industries. The higher costs have produced an abrupt decrease in income, especially in the poultry and pork sectors. If income continues to decrease, so will production, and the prices of chicken, turkey, pork, milk and eggs will increase.

They warn that the most devastating effects of increasing food prices will be felt especially in Third World countries.

Studies made by the Belgian Office of Scientific Affairs shows that biodiesel causes more health and environmental hazards because it creates a more pulverized pollution and releases more pollutants that destroy the ozone layer.

With regards to the argument claming that the agrifuels are harmless, Victor Bronstein, a professor at the University of Buenos Aires, has demonstrated that:

- It is not true that biofuels are a renewable and constant energy source, given that the crucial factor in plant growth is not sunlight but the availability of water and suitable soil conditions. If this were not the case, we would be able to grow corn or sugarcane in the Sahara Desert. The effects of large-scale production of biofuels will be devastating.
- It is not true that they do not pollute. Even if ethanol produces less carbon emissions, the process to obtain it pollutes the surface and the water with nitrates, herbicides, pesticides and waste, and the air is polluted with aldehydes and alcohols that are carcinogens. The presumption of a «green and clean» fuel is a fallacy.

The proposal of agrifuels is unviable, and it is ethically and politically unacceptable. But it is not enough just to reject it. It is necessary to implement a new energy revolution, but one that is at the service of the people and not at the service of the monopolies and imperialism. This is, perhaps, the most important challenge of our time, concludes Atilio Borón.

«The most devastating effects of increasing food prices will be felt especially in Third World countries»

«The proposal of agrifuels is unviable, and it is ethically and politically unacceptable. But it is not enough just to reject it. It is necessary to implement a new energy revolution»

As you can see, this summary took up some space. We need space and time; practically a book. It has been said that the masterpiece which made author Gabriel García Márquez famous, *One Hundred Years of Solitude,* required him to write fifty pages for each page that was printed. How much time would my poor pen need to refute those who for a material interest, ignorance, indifference or even for all three at the same time defend the evil idea and to spread the solid and honest arguments of those who struggle for the life of the species?

Some very important opinions and points of view were discussed at the Hemispheric Meeting in Havana. We should talk about those that brought us real-life images of cutting sugarcane by hand in a documentary film that seemed a reflection of Dante's Inferno. A growing number of opinions are carried by the media every day and everywhere in the world, from institutions like the United Nations right up to national scientific associations. I simply perceive that the debate is heating up. The fact that the subject is being discussed is already an important step forward.

Fidel Castro Ruz
May 9, 2007
5:47 p.m.

LESSONS WE LEARNED FROM THE 6TH HEMISPHERIC MEETING IN HAVANA

María Luisa Mendonça brought to the meeting in Havana, a powerful documentary film on the subject of manual sugarcane cutting in Brazil.

«Most of the wars in the last few decades have been waged over control of energy sources»

As I did in my previous reflection, I have written a summary using María Luisa's own paragraphs and phrases. It goes as follows:

We are aware that most of the wars in the last few decades have been waged over control of energy sources. Both in central and peripheral nations, energy consumption is guaranteed for the privileged sectors, while the majority of the world's population does not have access to basic services. The per capita consumption of energy in the United States is 13,000 kilowatts, while the world average is 2,429 and in Latin America the average is 1,601.

The private monopoly of energy sources is ensured by clauses in the bilateral or multilateral Free Trade Agreements.

The role of the peripheral nations is to produce cheap energy for the central wealthy nations, which represents a new phase in the colonization process.

It's necessary to demystify all the propaganda about the alleged benefits of agrifuels. In the case of ethanol, the growing

«The role of the peripheral nations is to produce cheap energy for the central wealthy nations, which represents a new phase in the colonization process»

and processing of sugarcane pollutes the soil and the sources of drinking water because it uses large amounts of chemical products.

Ethanol distillation produces a residue called vinasse. For every liter of ethanol produced, 10 to 13 liters of vinasse are generated. Part of this residue can be used as fertilizer, but most of it pollutes rivers and the sources of underground water. If Brazil were to produce 17 or 18 billion liters of ethanol per year, this means that at least 170 billion liters of vinasse would be deposited in the sugarcane field areas. Just imagine the environmental impact.

Burning sugarcane to facilitate the harvesting process, destroys many of the microorganisms in the soil, contaminates the air and causes many respiratory illnesses.

The Brazilian National Institute of Space Research issues a state of emergency almost every year in Sao Paulo –where 60% of Brazil's ethanol production takes place– because the burning-off has plunged the humidity levels in the air to extreme lows, between 13% and 15%; breathing is impossible during this period in the Sao Paulo area where the sugarcane harvest takes place.

The expansion of agrienergy production, as we know, is of great interest to the corporations dealing with genetically modified or transgenetic organisms, such as Monsanto, Syngenta, Dupont, Bass and Bayer.

In the case of Brazil, the Votorantim Corporation has developed technologies for the production of a non-edible transgenetic sugarcane, and we know of many corporations that are developing this same type of technology; since there are no measures in place to avoid transgenetic contamination in the native crop fields, this practice places food production at risk.

With regards to the denationalization of Brazilian territory, large companies have bought up sugar mills in Brazil: Bunge, Novo Group, ADM, Dreyfus as well as business magnates George Soros and Bill Gates.

As a result of all this, we are aware that the expansion of ethanol production has led to the expulsion of peasants from their lands and has created a situation of dependency on what we call the sugarcane economy, not because the sugarcane industry generates jobs, on the contrary, it generates unemployment because this industry controls the territory. This means that there is no room for other productive sectors.

At the same time, we are faced with the propaganda about the efficiency of this industry. We know that it is based on the exploitation of cheap and slave labor. Workers are paid according to the amount of sugar cane they cut, not according to the number of hours they have worked.

In Sao Paulo State where the industry is most modern –"modern" is relative of course– and it is the country's biggest producer, the goal for each worker is to cut between 10 to 15 tons of cane per day.

PEDRO RAMOS, a professor at Campinas University, made these calculations: in the 1980's, the workers cut around 4 tons a day and were paid the equivalent of more or less 5 dollars. Today, they need to cut 15 tons of sugarcane to be paid 3 dollars a day.

Even the Ministry of Labor in Brazil made a study which shows that before, 100 square

«The expansion of ethanol production has led to the expulsion of peasants from their lands and has created a situation of dependency on what we call the sugarcane economy»

«In the last five years, 1,383 sugarcane workers have died in Sao Paulo State alone»

meters of sugarcane yielded 10 tons; today, with transgenetic cane one must cut 300 square meters to reach 10 tons. Thus, workers must work three times more to cut 10 tons. This pattern of exploitation has resulted in serious health problems and even death for the workers.

A researcher with the Ministry of Labor in Sao Paulo says that in Brazil, sugar and ethanol are soaked in blood, sweat and death. In 2005, the Ministry of Labor in Sao Paulo reported the death of 450 worker for other causes such as murder and accidents –would this be because transportation to the refineries is very unsafe?– and also as a result of illnesses such as heart attack and cancer.

According to María Cristina Gonzaga, who carried out the survey, this Ministry of Labor research shows that in the last five years, 1,383 sugarcane workers have died in Sao Paulo State alone.

Slave labor is also common in this sector. Workers are usually migrants from the northeast or from Minas Gerais, lured in by intermediaries. Normally the contract is not directly with the company, but through intermediaries –in Brazil we call them «gatos»– who chose the laborers for the sugar mills.

In 2006, the district attorney's office of the Public Ministry inspected 74 sugar mills, only in Sao Paulo, and all of them were taken to court.

In March 2007 alone, the district attorney's office of the Ministry of Labor rescued 288 workers from slavery in Sao Paulo.

That same month, in Mato Grosso State, 409 workers were pulled out of a sugar mill that produces ethanol; among them was a group of 150 indigenous people. In Mato Grosso, the central area of the country, indigenous people are used as slave labor force in the sugar industry.

Every year, hundreds of workers suffer similar conditions in the fields. What are these conditions? They work without being legally reported, with no protective equipment, without adequate food or water, without access to washrooms and with very precarious housing; moreover, they have to pay for their housing and food, which is very expensive, and they also have to buy their implements such as boots and machetes and, of course, when work-related accidents occur, which is often, they do not receive adequate care.

For us, the central issue is the elimination of the latifundia because behind this modern façade we have a central issue, and that is the latifundia in Brazil and, of course, in other Latin American countries. Likewise, a serious food production policy is called for.

Having said this, I would like to present a documentary that we filmed in Pernambuco State with sugarcane workers; this is one of the biggest sugarcane producing regions, and so you will be able to see what the conditions are really like.

This documentary was made with the Pastoral Land Commission of Brazil (CPT) and with the unions of forestry workers in the state of Pernambuco.

With this, the outstanding and much admired Brazilian leader concluded her speech.

And now I shall present the opinions of the sugarcane cutters as they appeared in the film shown to us by María Luisa. In the documentary, when the people are not identified by name, they are identified as being a man, a woman or a young man. I am not including them all because there were so many.

SEVERINO FRANCISCO DE SILVA.- When I was 8 years old, my father moved to the Junco refinery. When I got there, I

«I work; every work is difficult, but sugarcane harvest is the worst work we have here in Brazil»

was about to turn 9; my father began to work and I was tying up the cane with him. I worked some 14 or 15 years in the Junco sugar mill.

A WOMAN.- I've been living at the sugar mill for 36 years. Here I was married and I gave birth to 11 children.

A MAN.- I've been cutting cane for many years, I don't even know how to count.

A MAN.- I started working when I was 7 and my life is that: cutting cane and weeding.

A YOUNG MAN.- I was born here, I'm 23 years old, and I've been cutting cane since I was 9.

A WOMAN.- I worked for 13 years here in Salgado Plant. I planted cane, spread fertilizer, cleaned sugarcane fields.

SEVERINA CONCEIÇĂO.- I know how to do all this field work: spread fertilizer, plant sugar cane. I did it all with a belly this big (she refers to her pregnancy) and with the basket beside me, and I kept on working.

A MAN.- I work; every work is difficult, but sugarcane harvest is the worst work we have here in Brazil.

EDLEUZA.- I get home and I wash the dishes, clean the house, do the house chores, do everything. I used to cut cane and sometimes I'd get home and I wasn't able to even wash the dishes, my hands were hurting with blisters.

ADRIANO SILVA.- The problem is that the foreman wants too much of us at work. There are days when we cut cane and get paid, but there are days when we don't get paid. Sometimes it's enough, and sometimes it isn't.

MISAEL.- We have a perverse situation here; the foreman wants to take off from the weight of the cane. He says that what we cut here is all that we have and that's that. We are working like slaves, do you understand? You can't do it like this!

MARCO.- Harvesting sugar cane is slave work, it's really hard work. We start out at 3 in the morning; we get back at 8 at night. It's only good for the boss, because he earns more every day that goes by and the worker loses, production decreases and everything is for the boss.

A MAN.- Sometimes we go to sleep without having washed, there's no water, we wash up in a stream down there.

A YOUNG MAN.- Here we have no wood for cooking, each one of us, if we want to eat, has to go out and find wood.

A MAN.- Lunch is whatever you can bring from home, we eat just like that, in the hot sun, carrying on as well as you can in this life.

A YOUNG MAN.- People who work a lot need to have enough food. While the boss of the sugar plantation has an easy life, with all the best of everything, we suffer.

A WOMAN.- I have gone hungry. I would often go to bed hungry, sometimes I had nothing to eat, nothing to feed my daughter with; sometimes I'd go looking for salt; that was the easiest thing to find.

EGIDIO PEREIRA.- You have two or three kids, and if you don't look after yourself, you starve; there isn't enough to live on.

IVETE CAVALCANTE.- There is no such thing as a salary here; you have to clean a ton of cane for eight reales; you earn according to whatever you can cut: if you cut a ton, you earn eight reales, there is no set wage.

A WOMAN.- A salary? I've never heard of that.

REGINALDO SOUZA.- Sometimes they pay us in money.

«Harvesting sugar cane is slave work, it's really hard work»

Nowadays they are paying in money; in the winter they pay with a voucher.

A WOMAN.- The voucher, well, you work and he writes everything down on paper, he passes it on to another person who goes out to buy stuff at the market. People don't see the money they earn.

JOSÉ LUIZ.- The foreman does whatever he wants with the people. What's happening is that I called for him to «calculate the cane», and he didn't want to. I mean: in this case he is forcing someone to work. And so the person works for free for the company.

CLOVIS DA SILVA.- It's killing us! We cut cane for half a day, we think we are going to get some money, and when he comes around to calculate we are told that the work was worth nothing.

NATANAEL.- The cattle trucks bring the workers here, it's worse than for the boss's horse; because when the boss puts his horse on the truck, he gives him water, he puts sawdust down to protect his hoofs, he gives him hay, and there is a person to go with him; as for the workers, let them do what they can: get in, shut the door and that's that. They treat the workers as if they were animals. The «Pro-Alcohol» doesn't help the workers, it only helps the sugarcane suppliers, it helps the bosses and they constantly get richer; because if it would create jobs for the workers, that would be basic, but it doesn't create jobs.

JOSÉ LOURENO.- They have all this power because in the House, state or federal, they have a politician representing these sugarcane mills. Some of the owners are deputies, ministers or relatives of sugar mill owners, who facilitate this situation for the owners.

A MAN.- It seems that our work never ends. We don't have holidays, or a Christmas bonus, everything is lost. Also, we don't even get a fourth of our salary, which is compulsory; it's what we use to buy clothes at the end of the year, or clothing for our children. They don't supply us with any of that stuff, and we see how every day, it gets much more difficult.

A WOMAN.- I am a registered worker and I've never had a right to anything, not even medical leaves. When we get pregnant, we have a right to a medical leave, but I didn't have that right, family guarantees; I also never got any Christmas bonus, I always got some little thing, and then nothing more.

A MAN.- For 12 years he's never paid the bonuses or vacations.

A MAN.- You can't get sick, you work day and night on top of the truck, cutting cane, at dawn. I became sick, and I was a strong man.

REINALDO.- One day I went to work wearing sneakers; when I swung the machete to cut cane, I cut my toe, I finished work and went home.

A YOUNG MAN.- There are no boots, we work like this, many of us work barefoot, the conditions are bad. They said that the sugar mill was going to donate boots. A week ago he cut his foot (he points) because there are no boots.

A YOUNG MAN.- I was sick, I was sick for three days, I didn't get paid, they didn't pay me a thing. I saw the doctor to ask for a leave and they didn't give me one.

A YOUNG MAN.- There was a lad who came from «Macugi». He was at work when he started to feel sick, and vomit. You need a lot of energy, the sun is very hot and people aren't made of steel, the human body just can't resist this.

«You can't get sick, you work day and night on top of the truck, cutting cane, at dawn. I became sick, and I was a strong man»

VALDEMAR.- This poison we use (he refers to the herbicides) brings a lot of illness. It causes different kinds of diseases: skin cancer, bone cancer, it enters the blood and destroys our health. You feel nauseous, you can even fall over.

A MAN.- In the period between harvests there is practically no work.

A MAN.- The work that the foreman tells you to do, must be done; because as you know, if we don't do it... We aren't the bosses; it's them that are the bosses. If they give you a job, you have to do it.

A MAN.- I'm here hoping someday to have a piece of land and end my days in the country, so that I can fill my belly and the bellies of my children and my grandchildren who live here with me.

Could it be that there is anything else?

End of the documentary.

There is nobody more grateful than I for this testimony and for María Luisa's presentation which I have just summarized. They make me to remember the first years of my life, an age when human beings tend to be very active.

I was born on a privately owned sugarcane latifundium bordering on the north, east and west on large tracts of land belonging to three American transnational companies which, together, possessed more than 600 thousand acres. Cane cutting was done by hand in green sugarcane fields; at that time we didn't use herbicides or even fertilizers. A plantation could last more than 15 years. Labor was very cheap and the transnationals earned a lot of money.

The owner of the sugarcane plantation where I was born was a Galician immigrant, from a poor peasant family, practically an illiterate; at first, he had been sent here as a soldier, taking the place of a rich man who had paid to avoid military

service and at the end of the war he was shipped back to Galicia. He returned to Cuba on his own like countless other Galicians who migrated to other countries of Latin America.

He worked as a hand for an important transnational company, the United Fruit Company. He had organizational skills and so he recruited a large number of day-workers like himself, became a contractor and ended up buying land with his accumulated profits in an area neighboring the southern part of the big American company. In the eastern end of the country, the traditionally independent-minded Cuban population had increased notably and lacked land; but the main burden of eastern agriculture, at the beginning of the last century, rested on the backs of slaves who had been freed a few years earlier or were the descendents of the old slaves and on the backs of Haitian immigrants. The Haitians did not have any relatives. They lived alone in their miserable huts made of palm trees, clustered in hamlets, with only two or three women among all of them. During the short harvesting season, cock-fights would take place.

The Haitians would bet their pitiful earnings and the rest they used to buy food which had gone through many inter-mediaries and was very expensive.

The Galician landowner lived there, on the sugarcane plantation. He would go out just to tour the plantations and he would talk to anyone who needed or wanted something from him. Often times he would help them out, for reasons that were more humanitarian than economic. He could make decisions.

The managers of the United Fruit Company plantations were Americans who had been carefully chosen and they were very well paid. They lived with their families in stately man-sions, in selected spots. They were like some distant gods, mentioned in a respectful tone by the starving laborers. They were never seen at the sugarcane fields where they sent their subordinates. The shareholders of the big transnationals lived in the United States or other parts of the world. The expenses of the plantations were budgeted and nobody could increase one single cent.

I know very well the family that grew out of the second marriage of that Galician immigrant with a young, very poor Cuban peasant girl, who, like him, had not been able to go to school. She was very self-sacrificing and absolutely devoted to her family and to the plantation's financial activities.

Those of you abroad who are reading my reflections on the Internet will be surprised to learn that that landowner was my father. I am the third of that couple's seven children; we were all born in a room in a country home, far away from any hospital, with the help of a peasant midwife, dedicated heart and soul to her job and calling upon years of practical experience. Those lands were all handed over to the people by the Revolution.

I should just like to add that we totally support the decree for nationalization of the patent from a transnational pharmaceutical company to produce and sell in Brazil an AIDS medication, Efavirenz, that is far too expensive, just like many others, as well as the recent mutually satisfactory solution to the dispute with Bolivia about the two oil refineries.

I would like to reiterate our deepest respect for the people of our sister nation of Brazil.

Fidel Castro Ruz
May 14, 2007
5:12 pm

THE UNANIMOUS OPINION

At the 6th Hemispheric Meeting in Havana, when the discussion turned to the subject of production of biofuels from foodstuffs, which are constantly getting more expensive, the huge majority voiced their opposition with indignation. But it was undeniable that some individuals with prestige, authority and good faith had been won over by the idea that the planet's biomass would suffice for both things in a relatively short time, mindless of the urgency to produce the foods, which are already scarce enough, that would be used as raw material for ethanol and agridiesel.

On the other hand, when the debate on the Free Trade Agreements with the United States began, several dozen people took part and all of them unanimously condemned both the bilateral and multilateral forms of such agreements with the imperialist power.

Taking into account the need for space, I shall return to the method of summarizing in order to present three eloquent speeches made by Latin American personalities who expressed extremely interesting concepts with great clarity and distinctiveness. As in all the summaries in previous reflections, the authors' exact manner of presentation is respected.

«NAFTA or the FTA of North America was merely the first step of something that it wants for the entire continent»

ALBERTO ARROYO (Mexico, Red mexicana de Acción contra el Libre Comercio-Mexican Action Network against Free Trade).

I would like to share with you the new plans of the empire and attempt to alert the rest of the continent about something new which is on the upswing or that is coming forward as a new strategy for a new phase of the United States' offensive. NAFTA or the FTA of North America was merely the first step of something that it wants for the entire continent.

The new attempt does not seem to take into account the defeat in the implementation of the FTAA, which even in it's Plan «B» recognizes that it cannot implement what it calls the comprehensive FTAA simultaneously in all the countries of the continent; it will try proceeding, piece by piece, negotiating bilateral Free Trade Agreements.

It succeeded in signing with Central America, but Costa Rica has not ratified it. In the case of the Andean nations, it has not even succeeded in sitting down at the bargaining table with all the countries, but only with two of them; and with these two it has not been able to conclude negotiations.

What is so new about the SPP (Security and Prosperity Partnership of North America)? I see three fundamental issues:

First: To strengthen military and security structures in order to confront the resistance of the peoples is precisely its reaction to the triumph of the movement that is jeopardizing its plans.

It is not a question of simply stationing military bases in danger zones or in areas with a high level of strategic natural resources, but trying to establish a close coordination, with plans concerted with the countries, in order to improve the security structures which are a way of confronting the social movements as if they were criminals.

This is the first novel aspect.

The second element, which also seems new to me: the principal actors in this entire neoliberal scheme were always directly the transnationals. The governments, particularly the United States government, were the spokesmen, the ones who formally carried out the negotiations, but really the interests that they were defending were directly those of the corporations. They were the great actors hidden behind the FTA and the FTAA project.

The novelty of the new SPP scheme is that these actors come out of the blue, take the foreground and the relationship is inverted: the corporate groups directly talking amongst themselves, in the presence of the governments that will then attempt to translate their agreements into policies, rule changes, changes of laws, etc. It was not enough for them now to privatize the public corporations; they are privatizing policy per se. The businessmen had never directly defined economic policy.

The SPP starts in a meeting, let's say it's called, «A meeting for the prosperity of North America»; they were tri-national meetings of businessmen.

Among the operative agreements being taken up by the SPP, one is the creation of tri-national committees by sectors, –what they call «captains of industry»– so that

«The governments, particularly the United States government, were the spokesmen, the ones who formally carried out the negotiations, but really the interests that they were defending were directly those of the corporations»

«They would like us never to know what was agreed to, they will only let us see fragments of the strategy, because it is never going to get translated into a complete text»

these define a strategic development plan of the sector in the North American region. In other words, Ford is multiplied or divided into three parts: that is, the Ford Corporation in the United States, the subsidiary of Ford in Mexico and the subsidiary of Ford in Canada decide the strategy for the auto industry sector in North America. It's the Ford Motor Company speaking to a mirror, with its own employees, with the directors of auto companies in Canada and in Mexico, to agree on a strategic plan that they will present to their governments which will translate and implement them into concrete economic policies.

There is a scheme to incorporate the security element; second point, to directly privatize the negotiations; and the third new aspect of this structure is perhaps, remembering a saying of our classic grandparents, that phrase of Engels where he was explaining that when the people are ready to take power through the mechanisms of formal democracy, like the zero on a thermometer or the 100, the rules of the game change: water will either freeze or boil, and even though we are speaking about bourgeois democracies, they will be first ones to break the rules.

The Free Trade Agreements have to go through congresses, and the fact is that it is getting more difficult to have them ratified by congresses, including the Congress of the empire, the United States Congress.

They are saying that this is not an international treaty therefore it doesn't have to get approved by the congresses. But, as it does touch on issues that disrupt the legal frame-

96

work in our countries, they will present in bit by bit; they will decide on a modification to legislation in a minute, and another one in the next minute; executive decrees to be implemented, changes in operative regulations, rules for standard functioning, but never the whole package.

Even though they were negotiated behind our backs and behind the backs of all peoples in general, sooner or later the Free Trade Agreements will be translated into a written text that will go to the congresses and then we will know what it was that they agreed to. They would like us never to know what was agreed to, they will only let us see fragments of the strategy, because it is never going to get translated into a complete text.

I shall close with a story so that we can realize the degree of sophistication, with regards to security, that these agreements and operative mechanisms of integration of security apparatuses have reached.

A short while ago, a plane took off from Toronto with tourists headed for a vacation in Puerto Vallarta, Mexico. While the plane was on the runway, the passenger list was examined again more carefully, and they discovered that there was someone there from Bush's list of terrorists.

As soon as the plane entered American air space –when you fly out of Toronto, American air space begins after you pass the Great Lakes and, in a jet, this takes a few minutes– two F-16s showed up flying alongside. They led the plane out of American air space and escorted it to Mexican territory where they forced it to land in the military section of the airport; then, they arrested this man and sent his family back.

You can imagine the impression those 200 poor tourists on the plane had, seeing the two armed F-16s flying alongside and rerouting the plane.

«One of the most devastating projects that have been proposed for the infrastructure, for the appropriation of our biodiversity, is the Puebla-Panama Plan, a strategy that not only appropriates our resources, but comes out of a military strategy of the empire»

Later, it turned out that he was not the terrorist that they thought, and they said to him: «Sorry, you can carry on with your vacation now, and make sure you call your family to come and join you».

JORGE CORONADO (Costa Rica, Continental Social Alliance)

The struggle against free trade in the region has various features. One of the most devastating projects that have been proposed for the infrastructure, for the appropriation of our biodiversity, is the Puebla-Panama Plan, a strategy that not only appropriates our resources, but comes out of a military strategy of the empire covering the territory from the south of Mexico right up to Colombia, passing through Central America.

In the struggle against hydroelectric dams which uproot and take by force the indigenous and peasant lands there have been cases where, using military repression, they have uprooted various native and peasant communities in the region.

We have the component of the struggle against the mining industry. Canadian, European and American transnationals have been pursuing this appropriation strategy.

We have been confronting the privatization of public services: electrical energy, water, telecommunications; the struggle in the peasant sector to defend seeds, against the patenting of living beings and against the loss of sovereignty to the transgenics.

98

We have been struggling against labor flexibility, one of the focuses oriented to the sector and, obviously, against the entire picture of dismantlement of our small scale peasant production.

Also, the struggle against the subject of intellectual property, which removes the use of generic medicines from our security, these being the main distribution focus which our social security institutes have in the region.

A central factor in this struggle against free trade has been against the Free Trade Agreements and, particularly, against the Free Trade Agreements with the United States, passed in Guatemala, Honduras, El Salvador and Nicaragua, through blood, sweat and tears. And this is not just a rhetorical expression.

In Guatemala, comrades in the struggle have been murdered while they have gone head to head against the treaty approvals. This struggle has allowed us to ensure a coordinating and mobilizing force for the greatest unity of the people's movement in the region.

In the case of the Honduran Parliament, the deputies walked out, breaking the minimum framework of institutional legality.

We have stated that, within the heart of the people's movement, this has not signified defeat. We have lost a battle, but it has allowed us to take a qualitative leap forward in terms of organization, unity and experience in the struggle against free trade.

The Popular Social Movement and the people of Costa Rica, which have prevented Costa Rica's approval of the

«We have been confronting the privatization of public services: electrical energy, water, telecommunications; the struggle in the peasant sector to defend seeds, against the patenting of living beings and against the loss of sovereignty to the transgenics»

«We are on the threshold of a fundamental stage in Costa Rica in terms of being able to prevent the advance of the neoliberal agenda; a defeat of this treaty would symbolically mean that we keep on adding up victories, like detaining and bringing FTA to a standstill»

FTA up until the present, forging unity with various academic, political and even business sectors to create a great national front of diverse and heterogeneous struggle, till now have succeeded in stopping the Costa Rican government, the right-wing neoliberals, and so they have not been able to approve the FTA. Today the possibility of a referendum in Costa Rica to decide the fate of the FTA is being proposed.

We are on the threshold of a fundamental stage in Costa Rica in terms of being able to prevent the advance of the neoliberal agenda; a defeat of this treaty would symbolically mean that we keep on adding up victories, like detaining and bringing FTA to a standstill.

Today we need solidarity in the popular movement, and we request it of the social and popular organizations which come to Costa Rica as international observers. The right-wing is preparing to encourage, if possible, a fraud that will guarantee it a win in the fight that is already lost, and having international observers from the popular movement will be an important contribution to active militant solidarity with our struggle.

Today, after a year, the FTA has not brought any more jobs, any more investments, or better conditions for the trade balance to any country in Central America. Today, in the entire region, we proclaim the slogan of agrarian reform, sovereignty and food security, as a central focus for our eminently agricultural nations.

Today, not just the United States but also Europe would like to appropriate one of the richest areas in biodiversity and natural resources. Today, more than ever, the coordinating focus of our different movements in the Central American region is to confront free trade in its multiple manifestations; hopefully this meeting will help give us coordinating elements, focuses for struggle and joint action that will allow us in this entire hemisphere to advance as one popular force.

We shall not rest in our efforts of organization and struggle until we reach the goal of a new world.

JAIME ESTAY (Chile, coordinator of REDEM –network of world economy studies– and, now professor at the University of Puebla in Mexico.

This crisis, in short, has to do with a manifest non-compliance with the promises that accompanied a group of reforms that began to be applied in Latin America in the 1980's.

Under the banner of free trade, we were told that we were going to achieve growth of our economies, that we were going to achieve diminished levels of inequality in our countries, along with diminished distances between our countries and the advanced world and, in brief, that we were going to achieve a move towards development in leaps and bounds. In some countries there was even talk about making those leaps and bounds into the First World.

In the matter of new integration or this open regionalism which took off more than 15 years ago, what was proposed was Latin American integration, or what we call Integration of Latin America, at the service of an opening-up process. A whole debate was set

«After a year, the FTA has not brought any more jobs, any more investments, or better conditions for the trade balance to any country in Central America»

«More than 15 years ago, what was proposed was Latin American integration, or what we call Integration of Latin America, at the service of an opening-up process»

up about how we had to integrate in order to open up, an integration that would not be the old-style protectionist integration, but an integration that would bring us better conditions to include ourselves in this global economy, in these markets which, supposedly, since they operated in a free manner, would produce the best possible results for our countries.

This relationship between integration and opening-up, that idea whose supreme objective of integration had to be the opening up of our countries, took place in effect; our countries effectively opened up and effectively and unfortunately the central theme of Latin American integration consisted in putting it at the service of this opening up.

Some officials were talking about what was called «the pragmatic phase of integration». We move forward as we are able; that more or less became the slogan. If what we need is to trade more, let us concentrate on trading more; if what we want is to sign a bunch of little agreements among countries, bilateral agreements or agreements between three or four countries, let us go in that direction, and at some point we shall be able to call this Latin American Integration.

The balance is clearly negative. I think that there is recognition, greater on various levels now, that what we have been calling the Integration of Latin America is not integration, it is trade; and it is not Latin American but a tangle of signed agreements between different countries of the region, none of which has lead to a process possessing an effectively Latin American character. The opening up, at whose service it is supposed that integration must be placed, has not produced any of the results that were announced in terms of economic growth, lessening of inequalities and achieving the sorely desired development that they said was supposed to be coming to us.

What we should point out is that we are witnessing an extreme deterioration of a style of integration that very clearly knew why, how and for whom integration was taking place.

In short, what I am talking about is an integration which was conceived on the foundations of neoliberalism, which has failed, both in terms of its own objectives and in terms of the objectives that we all have a right to demand and to expect in a genuine integration process.

The new Latin American integration was firmly supported by the policies and proposals coming from Washington. To a great extent, those American proposals have become something that will end up devouring its own offspring. Just the act of signing Free Trade Agreements has brought both the Andean community and the Central American Common Market to a crisis point.

An important part of the current crisis in Latin American integration has to do with the advance of the United States hemispheric project, not via the FTAA which managed to be stopped, but via the signing of different free trade treaties.

We can see the appearance of alternatives more clearly in the current panorama of integration. In many ways, ALBA (the Bolivarian Alternative for the Americas) is based on principles that are radically different from those belonging to that integration process which is in crisis.

«An integration which was conceived on the foundations of neoliberalism, which has failed, both in terms of its own objectives and in terms of the objectives that we all have a right to demand and to expect in a genuine integration process»

There are many functions left to define and many boundaries to be traced: the meaning of such concepts as «free trade», «national development», «market freedom», «food security and sovereignty», etc. What we are able to state is that we are witnessing, on the hemispheric and Latin American scene, a growing insurgency regarding the predominance of neoliberalism.

This is where the opinions expressed by these three personalities end, summing up the opinions of many of the participants in the debate about Free Trade Treaties. These are very solid points of view derived from a bitter reality and they have enriched my ideas.

I recommend my readers to pay attention to the complexities of human activity. It's the only way to see much further.

Space has run out. Today I should not add one more single word.

Fidel Castro Ruz
May 16, 2007
6:12 p.m.

THE ENGLISH SUBMARINE

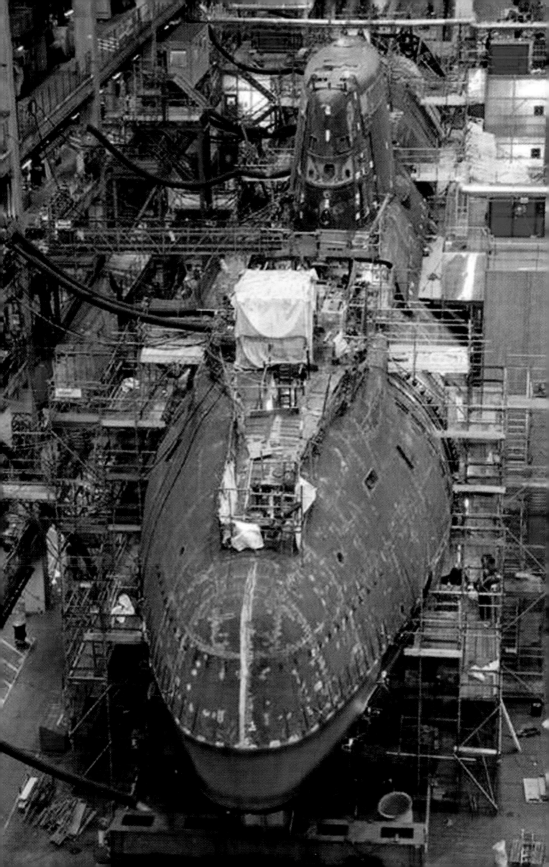

The press dispatches bring the news; it belongs to the Astute Class, the first of its kind to be constructed in Great Britain in more than two decades.

«A nuclear reactor will allow it to navigate without refuelling during its 25 year of service. Since it makes its own oxygen and drinking water, it can circumnavigate the globe without needing to surface,» was the statement to the BBC by Nigel Ward, head of the shipyards.

«It's a mean looking beast», says another.

«Looming above us is a construction shed 12 storeys high. Within it are 3 nuclear-powered submarines at different stages of construction,» assures yet another.

Someone says that «it can observe the movements of cruisers in New York Harbor right from the English Channel, drawing close to the coast without being detected and listen to conversations on cell phones». «In addition, it can transport special troops in mini-subs that, at the same time, will be able to fire lethal Tomahawk missiles for distances of 1,400 miles», a fourth person declares.

El Mercurio, the Chilean newspaper, emphatically spreads the news.

«The total cost of the three submarines, according to calculations that will certainly be below the mark, is 7.5 billion dollars (...) With such an amount of money, 75 thousand doctors could be trained to care for 150 million people»

The UK Royal Navy declares that it will be one of the most advanced in the world. The first of them will be launched on June 8 and will go into service in January of 2009.

It can transport up to 38 Tomahawk cruise missiles and Spearfish torpedoes, capable of destroying a large warship. It will possess a permanent crew of 98 sailors who will even be able to watch movies on giant plasma screens.

The new Astute will carry the latest generation of Block 4 Tomahawk torpedoes which can be reprogrammed in flight. It will be the first one not having a system of conventional periscopes and, instead, will be using fibre optics, infrared waves and thermal imaging.

«BAE Systems, the armaments manufacturer, will build two other submarines of the same class,» AP reported. The total cost of the three submarines, according to calculations that will certainly be below the mark, is 7.5 billion dollars.

What a feat for the British! The intelligent and tenacious people of that nation will surely not feel any sense of pride. What is most amazing is that with such an amount of money, 75 thousand doctors could be trained to care for 150 million people, assuming that the cost of training a doctor would be one-third of what it costs in the United States. You could build 3 thousand polyclinics, outfitted with sophisticated equipment, ten times what our country possesses.

Cuba is currently training thousands of young people from other countries as medical doctors.

In any remote African village, a Cuban doctor can impart medical knowledge to any youth from the village or from the surrounding municipality who has the equivalent of a grade twelve education, using videos and computers energized by a small solar panel; youth do not even have to leave their hometown, nor do they need to be contaminated with the consumer habits of a large city.

The important thing is the patients who are suffering from malaria or any other of the typical and unmistakable diseases that the student will be seeing together with the doctor.

The method has been tested with surprising results. The knowledge and practical experience accumulated for years have no possible comparison.

The non-lucrative practice of medicine is capable of winning over all noble hearts.

Since the beginning of the Revolution, Cuba has been engaged in training doctors, teachers and other professionals; with a population of less than 12 million inhabitants, today we have more Comprehensive General Medicine specialists than all the doctors in sub-Saharan Africa where the population exceeds 700 million people.

We must bow our heads in awe after reading the news about the English submarine. It teaches us, among other things, about the sophisticated weapons that are needed to maintain the untenable order developed by the United States imperial system.

We cannot forget that for centuries, and until recently, England was called the Queen of the Seas. Today, what remains of that privileged position is

«Cuba has today more Comprehensive General Medicine specialists than all the doctors in sub-Saharan Africa where the population exceeds 700 million people»

merely a fraction of the hegemonic power of her ally and leader, the United States.

Churchill said: Sink the Bismarck! Today Blair says: Sink whatever remains of Great Britain's prestige!

For that purpose, or for the holocaust of the species, is what his «marvellous submarine» will be good for.

Fidel Castro Ruz
May 21, 2007
5:00 p.m.

NOBODY WANTS TO TAKE
THE BULL BY THE HORNS

On March 28, less than two months ago, when Bush proclaimed his diabolical idea of producing fuel from food, after a meeting with the most important U.S. automobile manufacturers, I wrote my first reflection.

«The head of the empire was bragging that the United States was now the first world producer of ethanol, using corn as raw material»

The head of the empire was bragging that the United States was now the first world producer of ethanol, using corn as raw material. Hundreds of factories were being built or enlarged in the United States just for that purpose.

During those days, the industrialized and rich nations were already toying with the same idea of using all kinds of cereals and oilseeds, including sunflower and soy which are excellent sources of proteins and oils. That's why I chose to title that reflection: «More than 3 billion people in the world are being condemned to a premature death from hunger and thirst».

The dangers for the environment and for the human species were a topic that I had been meditating on for years. What I never imagined was the imminence of the danger. We as yet were not aware of the new scientific information about the celerity of climatic changes and their immediate consequences.

«To give humanity a respite and an opportunity to science and to the dubious good sense of the decision-makers, it is not necessary to take food away from two-thirds of the inhabitants of the planet»

On April 3, after Bush's visit to Brazil, I wrote my reflections about «The internationalization of genocide».

At the same time, I warned that the deadly and sophisticated weapons that were being produced in the United States and in other countries could annihilate the life of the human species in a matter of days.

To give humanity a respite and an opportunity to science and to the dubious good sense of the decision-makers, it is not necessary to take food away from two-thirds of the inhabitants of the planet.

We have supplied information about the savings that could be made simply by replacing incandescent light bulbs with fluorescent ones, using approximate calculations. They are numbers followed by 11 and 12 zeros. The first corresponds to hundreds of billions of dollars saved in fuel each year, and the second to trillions of dollars in necessary investments to produce that electricity by merely changing light bulbs, meaning less than 10 percent of the total expenses and a considerable saving of time.

With complete clarity, we have expressed that CO_2 emissions, besides other pollutant gases, have been leading us quickly towards a rapid and inexorable climatic change.

It was not easy to deal with these topics because of their dramatic and almost fatal content.

The fourth reflection was titled: «It is imperative to immediately have an energy revolution». Proof of the waste of energy in the United States and of the inequality of its distribution in the world is that in the year 2005, there were less

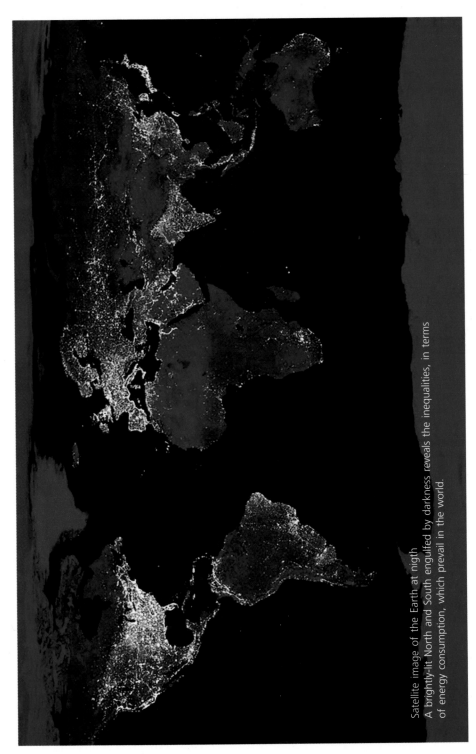

Satellite image of the Earth at nigth
A brightly-lit North and South engulfed by darkness reveals the inequalities, in terms of energy consumption, which prevail in the world.

«One of the richest territories in hydrocarbons, today suffers from a large deficit of oil and gas. According to Bush, these fuels must be extracted from foods, which are needed for the more and more hungry bellies of the poor of this Earth»

than 15 automobiles for each thousand people in China; there were 514 in Europe and 940 in the United States.

The last of these countries, one of the richest territories in hydrocarbons, today suffers from a large deficit of oil and gas. According to Bush, these fuels must be extracted from foods, which are needed for the more and more hungry bellies of the poor of this Earth.

On May Day 2006, I ended my speech to the people with the following words:

«If the efforts being made by Cuba today were imitated by all the other countries in the world, the following would happen:

«1st The proved and potential hydrocarbon reserves would last twice as long.

«2nd The pollution unleashed on the environment by these hydrocarbons would be halved.

«3rd The world economy would have a break, since the enormous volume of transportation means and electrical appliances should be recycled.

«4th A fifteen-year moratorium on the construction of new nuclear power plants could be declared».

Changing light bulbs was the first thing we did in Cuba, and we have cooperated with various Caribbean nations to do the same. In Venezuela, the government has replaced 53 million incandescent light bulbs with fluorescent in more than 95% of the homes receiving electrical power. All the other measures to save energy are being resolutely carried out.

Everything I am saying has been proven.

Why is it that we just hear rumors without the leadership of industrialized countries openly committing to an energy revolution, which implies changes in concepts and hopes about growth and consumerism that have contaminated quite a few poor nations?

Could it be that there is some other way of confronting the extremely serious dangers threatening us all?

Nobody wants to take the bull by the horns.

Fidel Castro Ruz
May 22, 2007
5:10 pm

FOR THE DEAF WHO
WON'T LISTEN

A summary of the FAO declaration from its headquarters in Rome, on May 16, 2007.

«It is forecast that the cereal import bill of the low-income food deficit countries will increase by about 25 percent in the current season»

World cereal production is on track to reach a record level in 2007. In spite of this, supplies will be barely adequate to meet increased demand, boosted by the development of the biofuels industry.

International prices for most cereals have risen significantly in 2006-07 and the current forecast shows that prices will stay high in 2007-08, according to the relevant report «Crop Perspectives and Food Situation». It is forecast that the cereal import bill of the low-income food deficit countries will increase by about 25 percent in the current season.

The rapid growth of the demand for maize-based ethanol is expected to increase by 9 percent the use of that grain in 2007-08.

Expectations for the world wheat harvest are down slightly since the April forecast.

In North Africa, a sharp decline is expected in 2007 cereal production, reflecting dry conditions in Morocco that are anticipated to halve the country's wheat production this year.

In Southern Africa, a reduced cereal harvest is expected for

«FAO recognizes the consequences of producing food-based fuels. That is something»

the second consecutive year. In Zimbabwe, a huge rise in the price of maize, a basic staple for millions, is anticipated as a result of the drought.

In Malawi, an ample exportable surplus will be available following a bumper harvest.

Emergency assistance is required for large numbers of vulnerable farmers in Bolivia affected by serious crop and livestock losses following drought and floods during the 2007 main cropping season.

The flare up of conflict in southern Somalia has displaced hundreds of thousands of people and is likely to reduce the area planted.

A first provisional FAO forecast for world production of rice in 2007 points to a slightly improved harvest with some 422 millions of tons, thus matching the 2005 record.

Except for China and India —the main producers— the cereal harvest totals in the rest of the countries will drop slightly.

FAO recognizes the consequences of producing food-based fuels. That is something.

But it is also remarkable to see the news that the United States Congress decided to replace 23 thousand incandescent light bulbs with fluorescent throughout its offices. It is said that American families, on their own volition, have decided to replace 37 million incandescent light bulbs with fluorescent. In just a few months, the 37 million replaced light bulbs will save the equivalent cost of gasoline for 260,000 automobiles. Calculate the savings when billions of incandescent light bulbs are replaced.

I shall digress now to tackle a topic which deals with my person, and I ask for your indulgence.

The news dispatches talk of an operation. My compatriots were not too happy that I explained on more than one occasion that my recovery would not be without its risks. Generally speaking, there was talk about a date when I would make a public appearance, dressed in my olive green fatigues as usual. Well then, it was not just one operation but several. Initially, it was not successful and this implicated a prolonged recovery period.

For many months, I relied on intravenous procedures and catheters for the greater part of my nutrition, and I wanted to spare our people an unpleasant disappointment. Today I receive everything required by my recovery orally. There is no danger greater than that related to age and to a state of health which I abused during some of the hazardous times I lived through. Nowadays I do what I should be doing, especially reflecting and writing about issues which, to my mind, have some importance and transcendence. I have a lot pending. For the present, I do not have time for films and photos that require me to constantly trim my hair, beard and moustache, and to get dressed up every day. Moreover, such presentations multiply requests for interviews. Let me simply say to everyone that my health has been improving and my weight is stable at around 80 kilos.

I try to keep the reflections as brief as possible so as not to take much space from the press and television news programs. The rest of the time I am reading, receiving information, talking on the phone with many other comrades and carrying out the rehab exercises that are necessary for my recovery. I cannot say

«Nowadays I do what I should be doing, especially reflecting and writing about issues which, to my mind, have some importance and transcendence»

or criticize everything that I know, because if I did so, human and international relations would be impossible, and our country cannot do without them. But I shall be true to the motto of never writing a lie.

Fidel Castro Ruz
May 23, 2007
5:06 p.m.

BUSH EXPECTS EVERYTHING TO BE SOLVED WITH A BANG

A word popped up in my mind. I looked it up in the dictionary and there it was; it's an onomatopoeic word and its connotation is tragic: bang. I've probably never used it in my life.

«One can never agree, in any kind of war, with events that take the lives of innocent civilians»

Bush is an apocalyptic person. I observe his eyes, his face and his obsessive preoccupation with pretending that everything he sees on the «invisible screens» are spontaneous thoughts. I heard his voice quaver when he answered criticism from his own father about his Iraq policy. He only expresses emotions and constantly feigns rationality. Of course he is aware of the impact of every phrase and every word on the public he addresses.

What's dramatic is that what he expects to happen may cost the American people many lives.

One can never agree, in any kind of war, with events that take the lives of innocent civilians. Nobody could justify the attacks of the German Air Force on British cities during World War II, nor the thousands of bombers that systematically destroyed German cities in the decisive moments of the war, nor the two atomic bombs which the United States

«Whom are they going to convince now that the thousands of nuclear weapons in their possession, the missiles and the precise and exact delivery systems they have developed are just to combat terrorism?»

dropped on Hiroshima and Nagasaki in an act of pure terrorism against old people, women and children.

Bush expressed his hatred of the poor world when he spoke on June 1, 2002 at West Point, of the pre-emptive attacks on «60 or more dark corners of the world».

Whom are they going to convince now that the thousands of nuclear weapons in their possession, the missiles and the precise and exact delivery systems they have developed are just to combat terrorism? Could it be perhaps that the sophisticated submarines being constructed by their British allies, capable of circumnavigating the globe without surfacing and reprogramming their nuclear missiles in mid-flight, will be used for that as well? I would never have imagined that one day such justifications would be used. Imperialism intends to institutionalize world tyranny with these weapons. It aims them at other great nations which arise not as military adversaries capable of surpassing their technology with weapons of mass destruction, but as economic powers that would rival the United States whose chaotic and wasteful consumerist economic and social system is absolutely vulnerable.

What's worse about the bang upon which Bush is hanging his hopes is the antecedent of his actions during the September 11th events, when, knowing full well that bloody attack on the American people was imminent, and having the capacity to foresee it and even to prevent it, he took off on a vacation with his entire administrative apparatus.

LONGEST US CONFLICTS

The Afghanistan and Iraq wars have become two of the longest military campaigns in the history of the United States.

Source:
US Defence Department.
World Encyclopedia

Wars the United States has been involved in	Duration (from date of declaration to intervention to treaty / ceasefire)	
Vietnam War (1964-79)	8 years, 5 months, 20 days	
War of Independence (1775-83)	8 years, 4 months, 15 days	
Afghanistan War (2001- present)*	5 years, 7 months	
Iraq War (2003-present)*	4 years, 1 month	
American Civil War (1861-65)	3 years, 11 months, 28 days	
Second World War (1941-45)	3 years, 8 months, 25 days	
Korean War (1950-53)	3 years, 1 month	
War of 1812 (1812-15)	2 years, 6 months, 21 days	
Mexican War (1846-48)	1 year, 8 months, 20 days	
First World War (1917-18)	1 year, 7 months, 5 days	
Spanish-Cuban-American War (1898)	7 months, 19 days	
Persian Gulf War (1991)	2 months, 25 days	

From the day of his appointment as President –thanks to the fraud orchestrated by his friends from the Miami mafia, in the manner of a «banana republic»– and prior to his inauguration, W. Bush was informed in detail of the same facts and in the same way as the president of the United States, who directed that he be informed. At that moment, the tragic events symbolized by the fall of the Twin Towers were still more than 9 months away.

If something similar were to happen with any kind of explosives or nuclear material, given that enriched uranium flows like water throughout the world since the days of the Cold War, what would be the probable fate of humanity? I try to remember and analyze many moments of humanity's march through the millennia, and I wonder: could my views be subjective?

Just yesterday Bush was bragging about having won the battle over his adversaries in Congress. He has a hundred

«What's worse about the bang upon which Bush is hanging his hopes is the antecedent of his actions during the September 11th events» billion dollars, all the money he needs to double, as he wishes, the number of American troops sent to Iraq, and to carry on with the slaughter. The problems in the region are increasingly aggravated.

Any opinion about the president of the United State's latest feats grows old in a matter of hours. Is it perhaps that the American people can't take this little moral fighting bull by the horns?

Fidel Castro Ruz
May 25, 2007
7:15 p.m.

IDEAS CANNOT BE KILLED

A few days ago, while analyzing the expenses involved in the construction of three submarines of the Astute series, I said that with this money «75,000 doctors could be trained to look after

«More than 600,000 people have lost their lives in Iraq and more than 2 million have been forced to emigrate since the American invasion began»

150 million people, assuming that the cost of training a doctor would be one-third of what it costs in the United States». Now, along the lines of the same calculations, I wonder: how many doctors could be graduated with the one hundred billion dollars that Bush gets his hands on in just one year to keep on sowing grief in Iraqi and American homes. Answer: 999,990 doctors who could look after 2 billion people that today do not receive any medical care.

More than 600,000 people have lost their lives in Iraq and more than 2 million have been forced to emigrate since the American invasion began.

In the United States, around 50 million people do not have medical insurance. The blind market laws govern how this vital service is provided, and prices make it inaccessible for many, even in the developed countries. Medical services feed into the Gross Domestic Product of the United States, but

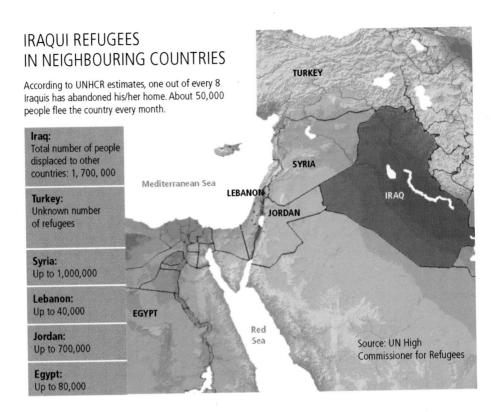

IRAQUI REFUGEES IN NEIGHBOURING COUNTRIES

According to UNHCR estimates, one out of every 8 Iraquis has abandoned his/her home. About 50,000 people flee the country every month.

Iraq:
Total number of people displaced to other countries: 1, 700, 000

Turkey:
Unknown number of refugees

Syria:
Up to 1,000,000

Lebanon:
Up to 40,000

Jordan:
Up to 700,000

Egypt:
Up to 80,000

Source: UN High Commissioner for Refugees

they do not generate conscience for those providing them nor peace of mind for those who receive it.

The countries with less development and more diseases have the least number of medical doctors: one for every 5,000, 10,000, 15,000, 20,000 or more people. When new sexually transmitted diseases appear such as AIDS, which in merely 20 years has killed millions of persons, –while tens of millions are afflicted, among them many mothers and children, although palliative measures now exist– the price of medications per patient could add up to 5,000, 10,000 or up to 15,000 dollars each year. These are fantasy figures for the great majority of Third World countries where the few public hospitals are overflowing with the ill who die piled up like animals under the scourge of a sudden epidemic.

To reflect on these realities could help us to better understand the tragedy. It is not a matter of commercial advertising that costs so much money and technology. Add up the starvation afflicting hundreds of millions of human beings; add to that the idea of transforming food into fuels; look for a symbol and the answer will be George W. Bush.

When he was recently asked by an important personality about his Cuba policy, his answer was this: «I am a hard-line President and I am just waiting for Castro's demise». The wishes of such a powerful gentleman are no privilege. I am not the first nor will I be the last that Bush has ordered to be killed; nor one of those people who he intends to go on killing individually or en masse.

«Ideas cannot be killed», Sarría emphatically said. Sarría was the black lieutenant, a patrol leader in Batista's army who arrested us, after the attempt to seize the Moncada Garrison, while three of us slept in a small mountain hut, exhausted by the effort of breaking through the siege. The soldiers, fuelled by hatred and adrenalin, were aiming their weapons at me even before they had identified who I was. «Ideas cannot be killed», the black lieutenant kept on repeating, practically automatically and in a hushed voice.

I dedicate those excellent words to you, Mr. W. Bush.

Fidel Castro Ruz
May 28, 2007
6:58 p.m.

THE G-8 MEETING

For those who are not informed –and I am one of them–, G-8 refers to the group of most developed countries, including Russia. The anticipated meeting which begins in 6 days has awakened great expectations due to the profound political and economic crisis threatening the world.

Let's read the news services.

The German news agency DPA announces that the German minister of Transportation and Urbanism, Wolfgang Tiefensee, declared «that the European Union countries have agreed on a common strategy».

«The European ministers of Urbanism meeting in the eastern city of Leipzig in an informal council under the motto of 'Urban Development and Territorial Cohesion', will employ a common strategy for the protection of the environment and the halting of climatic change».

«For example,» Tiefensee warned, «in the South of Europe the summer temperatures are expected to increase up to six degrees, while on the coasts we can expect strong winter storms.

«The drought threatening Spain and the lack of water in Poland are two more examples of the challenges facing the European Union, the German added at the end of the council».

Meanwhile, AFP reports that «the German minister of the environment, Sigmar Gabriel, judged it to be 'very difficult' that in the next G-8 summit any success could be achieved in the matter of climatic warming due to United States opposition».

«Germany will be the host country to the summit which will be held on June 6 to 8 in Heiligendamm with the eight most highly industrialized countries on the planet.

«Even though there are many in the United States who would like to see another kind of policy on climatic warming, 'unfortunately, Washington prevents' such a position to materialize, according to the German Social-Democratic minister.

«The German Chancellor, Angela Merkel, will put forth a 'strong signal' about the need to act urgently on this matter; the United States administration multiplies its opposition signals».

Reuters, the English agency, reports: «The United States has refused the German proposal to see that the Group of Eight agrees to tougher restrictions for carbon emissions that are producing global warming, according to the draft of the communiqué which will be presented at the meeting.

«The United States still has serious and fundamental concerns about this declaratory draft, to which Reuters had access.

«Treatment of climatic change goes completely counter to our position and crosses many 'red lines' in terms of which we simply cannot be in agreement, explained the American negotiators.

«This document is called FINAL, but we were never in agreement with any of the climatic language present in the text», they added.

«Germany would like an agreement to contain the increase of temperatures, in order to cut back global emissions by 50 percent lower than 1990 levels for the year 2050 and to increase energy efficiency by 20 percent for 2020.

RISING TEMPERATURES

The rise in temperatures could lead to much greater water and food shortages around the world.

Rising figures
Decreasing crops production and growing populations will place more people in serious risk of starvation.

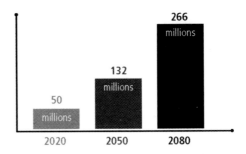

50 millions
2020

132 millions
2050

266 millions
2080

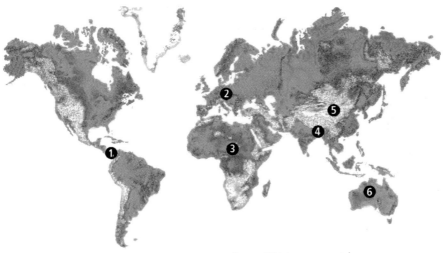

Source: UN Intergovernmental Panel on Climate Change, AP

❶ Latin America
- 2050: Decreased crop an livestock production

❷ Europe
- 2070: 16-44 million people will endure severe water shortages.

❸ Africa
- 2020: Agriculture dependent on rain could experince a 50 % drop in production
- 2080: Wheat crops could disappear altogether

❹ Bangladesh
- 2050: Rice production could drop by 10 %, wheat production by one third

❺ China
- 2050: A 3.6° C (6.5° F) rise in air temperature could reduce crop productions by 5-12 %

❻ Australia
- 2030: More droughts and forest fires, 30 % drop in agricultural production

«Washington rejects all those objectives».

While Blair declares that he would persuade his friend George, the only thing certain is that he added another submarine to the three that are now being built in Great Britain; with this, the expenses for sophisticated armament increases another 2.5 billion dollars. Perhaps someone with one of those new computer programs developed by Bill Gates could calculate the resources being used for war expenses at the cost of education, healthcare and culture for humanity.

George must say what he really thinks at the G-8 meeting, including the subject of the dangers threatening peace and food for human beings. Someone should ask him and he should not try to escape with the advice of his friend Blair.

Fidel Castro Ruz
May 29, 2007
6:45 p.m.

BUSH'S LIES AND CONS

don't like the idea of seeming to be a vengeful person, someone wishful to relentlessly pursue an adversary. I had promised myself to wait

«I wouldn't be the first or the last person that Bush would order or authorize his agents to remove»

a bit and see how the contradictions between Bush and his European allies would unfold on the vital subject of climate change. But George W. Bush went too far when he made a declaration that we read in an AP piece last Friday. The President of the United States stated that he would go to the Vatican «with a very open mind and…ready to listen» to the Pope, and he assured that they share a «common respect for human life and human dignity» and freedom.

«History has demonstrated that democracies don't go to war with each other and therefore the best way to reinforce peace is to promote freedom,» he added.

«This will be the American leader's first visit to Pope Benedict XVI. His last trip to Italy was in April 2005 for the funeral of Pope John Paul II», the agency reported.

In one of my reflections I said that I wouldn't be the first or the last person that Bush would order or authorize his agents to remove. Having seen his unusual declaration, I think that if Bush had ever read any history book, he would be aware that there, in Rome itself, an empire was born that nourished the vocabulary of political language for almost two thousand years; the Vatican City was also born there as time went by, after Constantine's Edict of Milan which officially removed obstacles to the practice of Christianity at the beginning of the fourth century A.D.

Historians tell us that the Caesar Nero who ordered the capital of the empire to be set on fire was heard to exclaim in satisfaction while the tragedy was in progress: «What a great poet is perishing!»

If only the historians were right! If only Bush were a poet! If only the inhabitants of the planet were those belonging to those times! If only nuclear, chemical, biological and mass destruction weapons did not exist! Even though it was a sad occurrence, including the death of the poet, who would be alarmed by a fire consuming what today would be just a great village?

Evidently Rome is not yet included among the 60 or more dark corners of the world that the United States military must be ready to pre-emptively attack, as Bush proclaimed at West Point on June 1, 2002.

Bush would now like to con Pope Benedict XVI. The Iraq War doesn't exist, it doesn't cost a cent, not one drop of blood has been spilled, nor have hundreds of thousands of innocent people died as part of a shameless bartering of lives for oil and gas, imposed by force of arms on the peoples of the Third World. Nor does the danger of another war against Iran exist, including possible tactical nuclear strikes to impose the same infamous formula. We are all required to believe that Russia does not feel threatened by a possible shower of annihilating and accurate nuclear missiles giving rise to a new and ever more dangerous arms race.

Following the chronic course of his rude lies, we might well wonder: why did Bush free an infamous, self-confessed terrorist like Posada Carriles on the same day that the 46th anniversary of the imperialist defeat at the Bay of Pigs was commemorated? Worse still, would he feel even a smidgen of pain about the injustice of keeping 5 Cuban heroes prisoners, some serving two life sentences, because they were informing their country about terrorist plans? Banish the thought that Bush didn't know who funded the countless assassination plots on Castro!

We have seen Bush making strange and disturbed grimaces while making official speeches to United States senators and representatives, boasting about the enemies he has had removed by issuing personal orders. He created official torture centers in Abu Ghraib and at the Guantánamo Naval Base; his agents, acting illegally, kidnapped people in many countries where CIA planes would secretly fly in, with or without permission from the corresponding authorities. Information would have to be extracted with well-studied physical torture methods.

How could he possibly think that Pope Benedict XVI would share values with him about respect for life, human dignity and freedom?

What does the Spanish language dictionary tell us?

Tall tale: an artfully disguised lie.

To con: to deceive, to hallucinate, taking advantage of someone's naiveté.

I promised brief reflections and I am keeping my word.

Fidel Castro Ruz
June 7, 2007
4:45 p.m.

THE TYRANT VISITS TIRANA

We now know that Bush's strange visit to the capital of Albania really happened. There he resolutely spoke in favor of independence for Kosovo without the least respect for the interests of Serbia, Russia and the various European countries, all sensitive to the fate of the province which was the scenario for the latest NATO war. He lectured Serbia that it would receive economic aid if it would support the independence of Kosovo, the birthplace of that country's culture. You can take it or you can leave it!

Bush is craving after affection. He fully enjoyed his reception without protests in Bulgaria. He spoke with that country's soldiers who took part in the wars in Iraq and Afghanistan. He tried to commit them further to spill generous blood in those peaceful wars.

When the leaders of the country complained about Bulgaria not being included under the protective umbrella against a nuclear strike, he immediately declared: you will have the necessary means to defend yourselves from medium range missiles.

From two thousand to five thousand of Bush's soldiers will be rotating constantly through the three military bases implanted by the empire in Bulgaria. As if we were living in the happiest of all worlds!

Fidel Castro Ruz
June 11, 2007
6:00 p.m.

153

NEEDING AFFECTION

WANTED
George W. Bush

FOR CRIMES AGAINST
HUMANITY AND THE PLANET

Beware if you meet this man!
He suffers from delusions that he is the democratically
elected President of the USA.
Do not approach him, he is nuclear armed and
dangerous.
Act responsibly and contact the nearest police station.

http://www.motherearth.org/bushwanted

Albania was really the only place where Bush got any affection; to such an extent that the reception in Bulgaria where several thousand people awaited him waving little American flags seemed cool to him.

Bush's support for Albania's immediate entry into NATO and his decision to demand independence for the province of Kosovo made quite a few Albanians a bit crazy.

Newspapers and other media report that some of them, when questioned individually, answered:

«Bush is a symbol of democracy. The United States is a protector of peoples' freedom».

Thousands of unarmed Albanian soldiers and policemen, because that was what the Yankee authorities demanded, stood guard in two columns along more than 20 kilometers stretching between the airport and the capital.

The thorny problem of the independence of one part of Serbia is very controversial in Europe, and a precedent that could be followed in several countries by other regions claiming sovereignty within current borders.

And so Albania went over from the extreme left to the extreme right.

To live to see it! Seeing is believing!

Serbia receives a hard blow not only political but also economic. Kosovo possesses 70 percent of Serbia's energy reserves. Between 1928 and 1999, the year of the NATO war against Serbia, the province contributed 70 percent of the zinc and silver. It is estimated to have 82 percent of its possible reserves of these metals. It also has the largest reserves of bauxite, nickel and cobalt.

Serbia loses factories, lands and properties, and is left only with the duty to pay for the foreign debt incurred for investments in Kosovo prior to 1998.

I have just received a news dispatch from AFP that forces me to extend myself for a few more lines. It literally reads:

«Moscow, June 13, 2007.

«Russia accuses the West of holding secret talks for the independence of Kosovo.

«Russia reproached the Western nations on Wednesday for working secretly and 'unilaterally' to prepare Kosovo's independence, according to a communiqué released by the Russian Ministry of Foreign Relations.

«The 'secret discussions lead us to suspect that a scenario for Kosovo's sovereignty is being unilaterally prepared', indicated the Ministry's spokesman, Mikhail Kamynin, in reference to the meeting that the Western powers held in Paris on Tuesday, in the absence of the Moscow government.

«This attitude, he continued, is 'intolerable'; moreover, 'Russia was not invited to the meeting, and this is incompatible with declarations in the sense of seeking accommodating solutions', he added».

Fidel Castro Ruz
June 13, 2007
8:12 p.m.

THEY WILL NEVER HAVE CUBA
REFLECTION AND MANIFESTO
FOR THE PEOPLE OF CUBA

hope that no-one say that I am gratuitously attacking Bush. Surely they will understand my reasons for strongly criticizing his policies.

Robert Woodward is an American journalist and writer who became famous for the series of articles published by

«Bush was betrayed by his subconscious. It was in his mind when he declared what scores of dark corners should be expecting to happen and Cuba occupies a special place among those dark corners»

The Washington Post, written by him and Carl Bernstein, and which eventually led to the investigation and resignation of Nixon. He is author and co-author of ten best-sellers. With his fearsome style he manages to wrench confessions from his interviewees. In his book, *State of Denial,* he says that on June 18, 2003, three months after the Iraq war had begun, as he was on the way out of his White House office following an important meeting, Bush slapped Jay Garner on the back and said to him:

«*Hey, Jay, you want to do Iran?*

«Sir, the boys and I talked about that and we want to hold out for Cuba. We think the rum and the cigars are a little better...The women are prettier».

Bush laughed. «You got it. You got Cuba».

«It will very soon be 50 years since our people started suffering a cruel blockade; thousands of our sons and daughters have died or have been mutilated as a result of the dirty war against Cuba»

Bush was betrayed by his subconscious. It was in his mind when he declared what scores of dark corners should be expecting to happen and Cuba occupies a special place among those dark corners.

Garner, a recently retired three-star General who had been appointed Head of the Post-War Planning Office for Iraq, created by secret National Security Presidential Directive, was considered by Bush an exceptional man to carry out his war strategy. Appointed for the post on January 20, 2003, he was replaced on May 11 of that same year at the urging of Rumsfeld. He didn't have the nerve to explain to Bush his strong disagreements on the matter of the strategy to be pursued in Iraq. He was thinking of another one with identical purpose. In the past few weeks, thousands of marines and a number of US aircraft carriers, with their naval supporting forces, have been maneuvering in the Persian Gulf, a few miles off the Iranian territory.

It will very soon be 50 years since our people started suffering a cruel blockade; thousands of our sons and daughters have died or have been mutilated as a result of the dirty war against Cuba, the only country in the world to which an Adjustment Act has been applied inciting illegal emigration, yet another cause of death for Cuban citizens, including women and children; more than 15 years ago Cuba lost her principal markets and sources of supply for foods, energy, machinery, raw materials and long-term low-interest financing.

First the socialist bloc collapsed followed almost immediately by the USSR, dismantled piece by piece. The empire tightened and internationalized the blockade; the proteins and calories which were quite well distributed despite our deficiencies were reduced approximately by 40 percent; diseases such as optical neuritis and others appeared; the shortage of medicines, also a result of the blockade, became an everyday reality. Medicines were allowed to enter only as a charitable act, to demoralize us; these, in their turn, became a source of illegal business and black-market dealings.

Inevitably, the «special period» struck. This was the sum total of all the consequences of the aggression and it forced us to take desperate measures whose harmful effects were bolstered by the colossal media machine of the empire. Everyone was awaiting, some with sadness and others with oligarchic glee, the crumbling of the Cuban Revolution.

The access to convertible currency greatly harmed our social consciousness, to a greater or a lesser degree, due to the inequalities and ideological weaknesses it created.

Throughout its lifetime, the Revolution has taught the people, training hundreds of thousands of teachers, doctors, scientists, intellectuals, artists, computer engineers and other professionals with university and post-graduate degrees in dozens of professions. This storehouse of wealth has allowed us to reduce infant mortality to low levels, unthinkable in any Third World country, and to raise life expectancy as well as the average educational level of the population up to the ninth grade.

By offering Cuba oil under favorable terms of payment at a time when oil prices were escalating dramatically, the Venezuelan Bolivarian Revolution brought a significant relief and opened up new possibilities, since our country was already beginning to produce her own energy in ever-growing amounts.

Concerned over its interests in that country, the empire had for years been planning to destroy that Revolution, and so it attempted to do it in April 2002, as it will attempt to do

«Cuba will continue to develop and improve the combative capacities of her people, including our modest but active and efficient defensive weapons industry»

again as many times as it can. This is why the Bolivarian revolutionaries are preparing to resist.

Meanwhile, Bush has intensified his plans for an occupation of Cuba, to the point of proclaiming laws and an interventionist government in order to install a direct imperial administration.

Based on the privileges granted to the United States in Bretton Woods and Nixon's swindle when he removed the gold standard which placed a limit on the issuing of paper money, the empire bought and paid with paper tens of trillions of dollars, more than twelve digit figures. This is how it preserved an unsustainable economy. A large part of the world currency reserves are in US Treasury bonds and bills. For this reason, many would rather not have a dollar crisis like the one in 1929 that would turn those paper bills into thin air. Today, the value of one dollar in gold is at least eighteen times less than what it was in the Nixon years. The same happens with the value of the reserves in that currency.

Those paper bills have kept their low current value because fabulous amounts of increasingly expensive and modern weapons can be purchased with them; weapons that produce nothing. The United States exports more weapons than anyone else in the world. With those same paper bills, the empire has developed a most sophisticated and deadly system of weapons of mass destruction with which it sustains its world tyranny.

Such power allows it to impose the idea of transforming foods into fuels and to shatter any initiative and commitment to avoid global warming, which is visibly accelerating.

Hunger and thirst, more violent hurricanes and the surge of the sea is what Tyranians and Trojans stand to suffer as a result of imperial policies. It is only through drastic energy savings that humanity will have a respite and hopes of survival for the species; but the consumer societies of the wealthy nations are absolutely heedless of that.

Cuba will continue to develop and improve the combative capacities of her people, including our modest but active and efficient defensive weapons industry which multiplies our capacity to face the invaders no matter where they may be, and the weapons they possess. We shall continue acquiring the necessary materials and the pertinent fire power, even though the notorious Gross Domestic Product as measured by capitalism may not be growing, for their GDP includes such things as the value of privatizations, drugs, sexual serv-ices and advertising, while it excludes many others like free educational and health services for all citizens.

From one year to the next the standard of living can be improved by raising knowledge, self-esteem and the dignity of people. It will be enough to reduce wastage and the economy will grow. In spite of everything, we will keep on growing as necessary and as possible.

«Freedom costs dearly, and it is necessary to either resign ourselves to live without it or to decide to buy it for its price», said Martí.

«Whoever attempts to conquer Cuba will only gather the dust of her soil soaked in blood, if he does not perish in the fight», exclaimed Maceo.

We are not the first revolutionaries to think that way! And we shall not be the last!

One man may be bought, but never a people.

Fate decreed that I could survive the empire's murderous machine. Shortly, it will be a year since I became ill and, while I hovered between life and death, I stated in the Proclamation of July 31, 2006: «I do not harbor the slightest doubt that our people and our Revolution will fight until the last drop of blood».

Mr. Bush, don't you doubt that either!
I assure you that you will never have Cuba!

Fidel Castro Ruz
June 17, 2007
2:03 p.m.

Imprenta
Federico
Engels